I Remember. . . .

May God bless you.

Larissa W. Holt
May 13, 2010

The photo on the cover is of my father, Leanid Nossov, my mother, Klaudia Nossowa, and me, Lorissa Nossowa, taken before World War II. The story of how Mother was able to save this priceless family photo is found on pages 236-238.

Long after Mother came to America, she continued to use her artwork to set herself free; the black memories of her past would not release her. In the drawings on the cover and elsewhere in the book she depicted the *Straflager* (prison camp) outside Grajevo, Poland, where she was held 1942-1944.

LWH

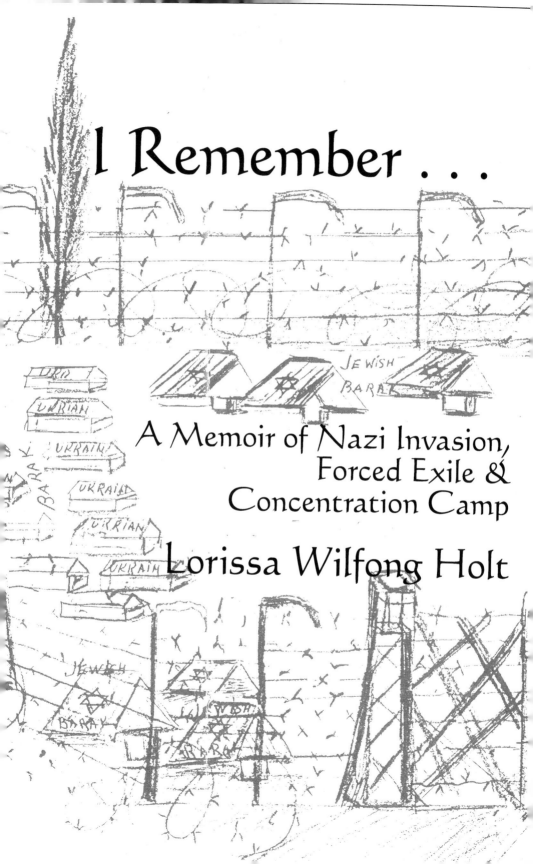

I Remember . . .

A Memoir of Nazi Invasion, Forced Exile & Concentration Camp

Lorissa Wilfong Holt

I Remember. . . . A Memoir of Nazi Invasion, Forced Exile & Concentration Camp

International Standard Book Number (ISBN):
978-0-9702761-0-0

Printed in the United States

Cover and Book Design by Gary Richardson

Edited by Jean Terra

Published by Book Lore Publications
3223 N 36 St #3
Boise ID 83703-4699

Also by Lorissa Wilfong Holt:
A Gift of Life: A Memoir of a Peace Corps Volunteer in Hungary (2003)

Dedication

I dedicate this book to all
my children and all my
grandchildren,
To my brother, Ed Merohn, his
wife and their two sons,
To my kind and loving husband,
Burt Holt, who stood by me all
through my writing process.
In remembrance of my mother,
Klaudia Nossowa Marohn and
my wonderful grandparents Vasil
and Ephrosenia Chomenko.

Contents

Acknowledgments

I want to thank my friend Agnes Smith, who kept me writing from the beginning of my project when writing and recollecting was difficult.

I want to thank Lorry Roberts for being my advisor/agent and for being there when I needed her the most. It was a lucky day when I met Lorry Roberts many years ago. Lorry has been instrumental in connecting me with the nicest people from the publishing world.

I want to thank Gary Richardson, a kind and helpful man, who designed the cover and interior of my book.

Most of all, I want to thank Jean Terra for all her excellent editing, patience and understanding. Jean Terra is one of the best editors in Idaho. I thank her for many unselfish hours of dedicated work on my manuscript.

Preface

For a long time, I resisted telling my story. It had been a lifetime since I had allowed myself to think about those terrible days of World War II. I was reluctant to dredge up all those painful memories, to revisit those terrible days and relive those events now so long in the past.

I was just a young child, not quite eight years old, when my mother, Klaudia, and I were taken by German soldiers from our home in Kiev, Ukraine, and shipped off in cattle cars to the Nazi work camps. In late 1944, we were moved to Dachau where we had not much hope of survival. I was near death when the Americans liberated this infamous death camp on April 29, 1945.

During the war and for years afterward, night after night, I had terrifying nightmares that would not let me sleep. In one that recurred often, a Nazi soldier pointing a bayonet-mounted rifle at me, chased me for hours over the glass-topped roof of a greenhouse. No matter how fast I ran, I never could get away from my attacker.

With each step, my feet broke through the glass panes. My legs were cut and bleeding. As I ran, I looked over my shoulder and saw the pools of my blood that I was leaving behind.

I felt agonizing pain in my lungs and in my legs. The cruel Nazi kept gaining on me. At times, my enemy was so close I could feel his hot breath on the nape of my neck. When I looked into his face, I saw that it was always the same Nazi soldier who had pierced my thigh with a bayonet in the Dachau Concentration Camp.

The murderous race went on until, breathless with exhaustion, I was able to fight my way out of the nightmare. I would sit up on the edge of the bed with my heart pounding and my nightgown wet with perspiration.

After I came to America, little by little, my nightmares subsided. I was reluctant to begin writing this book because I feared this would start my agony all over again

And I doubted my ability to remember. I was a very young child when most of these events took place and I was now a woman in her seventies attempting to write about them.

But I finally accepted that my story was one that needed to be told and it was one that only I could tell.

I wanted to leave a legacy of words and memories for my children and my grandchildren. I want them to know how hard it was for my grandparents, my mother and me to survive from one day to the next during the Nazi occupation of our country.

I want them to understand the cruel insanity of World War II and the life and death struggles that I and so many others endured during those terrible times. The Holocaust resulted in the death of six million Jews, and the Nazis also enslaved and murdered several million of my Ukrainian countrymen. We must never forget nor allow future generations to forget these historical facts.

And so, with encouragement from friends and family, I began what seemed, at the time, to be a huge and insurmountable task. Memories began flooding my mind and, through the long and patient process of writing, my mind began to unlock its secrets.

In truth, I think I was preparing to write my story long before I could admit it to myself. During my early married years, I never allowed myself to read or see movies about the Holocaust and World War II. It was my subconscious effort to shield myself from pain.

I now believe this also was a way for me to keep my memories pure and unadulterated by the thoughts and experiences of others who had endured many of the same horrific events that I had. I wanted my story to be told as I lived it and as I remembered it from the earliest recollections of my innocent childhood and through the downward-spiraling of my life through those tragic days.

I have not always remembered exact dates but I do vividly remember specific events that were marked by the changing seasons of the year, by birthdays and by holidays, and so I have been able to reconstruct those years.

All accounts in this book are true. I witnessed the suffering. I felt the starvation and I heard the piercing cries for help. I mourned the dying and I helped to bury them. I felt a profound sorrow in my heart for what I witnessed and for what I experienced.

I also want to pass on my grandfather's special legacy of hope and to share his words, his thoughts and ideas that will help his descendants to know what a great and loving man he was. I hope my children will understand how, through hardships and pain, our family became closer and more loyal, how our love for each other increased beyond all measure during the most dangerous time of our lives.

I hope that through my book, *I Remember....*, memories will continue to be passed down in our family from one generation to the next long after I am gone.

Often I ask myself, "Why did I survive when others died like flies all around me?" I was not the strongest, nor the wisest, nor the bravest; I was the youngest and most vulnerable. So why was I spared? Was it fate or God or just the luck of the draw? I was raised in a secular society where God was either unmentioned or discredited. How could a just God, if there was such a being, choose to save one unfortunate creature and allow so many others to perish?

Now that I am a Christian, I do thank God for sparing my life but I still do not quite understand why I survived. Perhaps, in the telling of my story, the voices of those who perished and are not here to speak for themselves will now be heard.

I am grateful to be alive even though survivor's guilt haunts me to this day. I find that I am deeply sympathetic to the sufferings of man and beast alike, to those who are hungry, who feel great pain, and who survive much loss. I can relate to their suffering now because I remember my past.

Above all, I am thankful that my wandering days are over and I am home at last!

Lorissa Wilfong Holt
October 2007

I Remember. . . .

Part One
Nazi Invasion

I. My Early Carefree Years

What do I remember? I often asked myself. What are my earliest recollections? Once, in my journal, I recorded from my memory a story called *Strawberries and Bees*. Later on, as I read and reread that story, I came to the conclusion that this was my earliest recollection.

I was six years old when I was sent to a summer camp somewhere in the forest on the outskirts of Kiev, Ukraine. It was one of those Communist Youth Camps where children, at an early age, were gently introduced to communist philosophy in the pleasant setting of summer camp.

I remember one afternoon quite clearly. In fact, that day was burned into my mind forever. All the children were seated around an oblong table in the shade of huge trees eating bright-red strawberries with sugar and cream. Oh, they were so good! I have never eaten better tasting strawberries since. There were bees buzzing around and feasting on the crumbs of sugar and drops of cream on the table. Most of the children were minding their own business and enjoying the afternoon snack. But not me! I was on a mission. Armed with a large serving spoon, I was whacking away the bees. I think I believed that I was protecting my friends, myself and our delicious afternoon snack from the marauding insects.

The next thing I remember was seeing two pairs of stout legs standing almost over me while I was lying on my back in a creek. As my eyes moved upward, I saw two nurses in white uniforms with a red cross on their white caps. It was easy to see by the grim look on their faces and by the way they had folded their arms under their ample bosoms that they were angry with me. It was obvious to me, I was in big trouble!

One of the nurses was pointing at me and telling the other children, "You must never, never, do what Lorissa just did."

The younger nurse knelt beside me in the creek and with a gentle touch poured cool water over my bee-stung and swollen lips, neck, shoulders, arms and hands. The cold water was like a gift from heaven that relieved my stinging pain.

That same day I was sent home. The next thing I remembered was the familiar, concerned faces of my grandparents. They were lovingly tending to my bee stings. Even though I was quite young, I remember that episode so vividly. Who could ever forget such a painful experience?

I remember staying with my grandparents during the summers when I was about seven. Usually, I spent my summers and holidays during the school year with my grandparents. My mother had to work and my grandparents felt that I would be much safer in their home than being in an apartment all by myself. Their home was nice and clean. There were all sorts of fun things to do and good things to eat. Each day brought new adventures.

While Grandmother was busy in the kitchen, Grandfather and I enjoyed doing chores outdoors. In the mornings, we walked several blocks to buy a daily newspaper. In early spring, Grandfather bought a bunch of fresh blue violets for Grandmother. Other times, we went to the grocery store for things Grandmother needed.

There was a kitchen garden to work in and juicy sweet berries to pick. It did not matter what we did, as long as Grandfather and I were together. Most of the time, we were inseparable.

I remember that afternoons usually were a quiet time for my grandparents and an extremely boring time for me. My grandfather read the daily newspaper and took a nap while Grandmother was doing quiet work, sewing or reading or writing letters. Left to my own devices, I spent those hours in my own bedroom where I had books, paper, pencils and dolls. On one afternoon I lost all interest in those things and kept looking at myself in the mirror.

I loved to sit in front of a mirror and comb my hair, arranging it in many different styles. As I was playing with my hair, I noticed a pair of scissors at my elbow—scissors had a habit of getting me into trouble. I always thought my forehead was too high and these scissors presented me with a chance to do something about it. So, very carefully, I combed out a section of hair over my forehead, closed my eyes and took a quick snip. Unfortunately, it was not a straight cut, way too short on the left side.

Even as a child, I had a stubborn nature. Nothing stopped me once I had committed myself to a task. I took another quick snip. This time it was much too short on the right side.

After several more snips, to my dismay, I ran out of hair! I looked into the mirror and saw a little girl with long blond hair in the back and a short crew cut where my bangs should have been. Tears filled my eyes, blurring my image in the mirror. But this was no time to cry. I knew I was in big trouble. Mother was coming to get me that evening and I needed to look for a hiding place.

Quickly I scooted under my grandparents' high bed and hid behind some of Grandmother's sewing baskets. I held my breath when I heard Mother coming in. She soon found me and, with horror, she saw what I had done to myself. Once again, I felt the wrath of that old wooden spoon on my backside. Mother was not a religious person like Grandmother but she strongly believed in one Bible verse, "...spare a rod and spoil the child" (Proverbs 13:24). It was well and good for her to quote the Bible; she did not have red welts on her backside. It did not hurt her when she sat on a hard chair or even on a soft bed.

My childish antics extended to other areas of interest in my life. I liked to sew new clothes for my dolls, just like Grandmother sewed for me. My favorite place to play with the dolls was on the floor of my mother's closet. Mother and I shared a room in my grandparents' house, and I pretended that the closet was a large doll house. One day, as I was sewing a new outfit for my favorite doll, I ran out of the fabric scraps Grandmother had given me that afternoon. I wanted to make a full skirt, not something tight and skimpy.

Looking around in the dark closet, I saw something that looked like a doll's skirt dangling over my head. Without a moment's hesitation, I grabbed my scissors and cut off the ruffled black lace end of a sleeve from my mother's dress. It never occurred to me that I had done something wrong until later that evening when I heard my mother's angry voice mixed with sobs cry out, "Who cut off the sleeve off my new dress? I planned to wear it to the opera to-night. Where is Lorissa? Where is she?" If ever there was an emergency, this was it! I knew I needed a better hiding place. Suddenly, I remembered how Grandfather and I used to play hide-and-go-seek with the help of his old grandfather clock a long time ago. But now, the old clock seemed smaller. I had to scrunch up tightly into a small ball in order to fit into the lower part of the clock and shut the door. Immediately, the heavy brass pendulum started to scrape across the base of my neck. With every tick-tock, as it moved back and forth, I thought I would lose my head and images of Marie Antoinette drift-ed before my eyes.

Eventually, my mother found me. But this time, the luck was with me; stained and chipped from years of double duty, the old wooden spoon broke after a few strong whacks. Next morning, the sun was shining and everything was good again.

Such were the good and happy days of my child-hood. Our lives were modest and simple but happy.

Even the worst of those early days was not so bad compared to what was soon to come. Already the changes were taking place. Worry was etched on the faces of my dear grandparents and on the faces of their good friends who were like aunts and uncles to me. Rumors of war and of troubled times to come were everywhere. Food rationing was now strictly enforced. Extra food was impossible to buy at any price, not even on the black market. All this was happening even before Kiev fell into Nazi hands.

2. About Our Family

I remember the many stories I was told about my grandparents when they were young. Vasil and Ephrosenia Chomenko built a nice two-story brick house at #48 New Koravaevka Street. Their three children were born in their nice new home. Friends often joked that a new baby was born to the Chomenkos every three years.

Their first child, a girl, was born in 1907, and they named her Pasha. Three years later, in 1910, a second child was born, my mother, Klaudia. Three years later, in 1913, a long awaited son was born. The baby was premature and lived less than twenty-four hours. My poor grandmother and grandfather were heartbroken. They could not talk about the son they had wanted so much and who would have carried the Chomenko name into the next generation.

Once in a while, Grandmother would say, "My baby boy was a beautiful child." Then, she would break down and cry for hours. Grandfather did not say much about the son he had so hoped for; he kept all that pain and sorrow buried deep in his heart.

Aunt Pasha married a man by the name of Uharov (I don't remember his first name) who during the war was a low-ranking officer in the Russian Army. They had a son named Urie who was much younger than I. Once, Aunt Pasha, her husband and little Urie came to visit us in Kiev but I was too young to remember that visit.

When Mother was twenty-one, she married Leanid Nossov who worked as an electrical engineer on the Dnieper River Dam in Kiev. For three years, they were blissful newlyweds, spending every waking moment with each other. On March 15, 1934, I entered into their private world and, according to Mother, shattered it. I am sad to say that Mother was unhappy about her pregnancy and even more miserable after I was born. I heard her tell countless times of how she had tried to kick me off the delivery table but, to her dismay, the nurses stopped her.

In 1939, during the second wave of the Communist Terror in Ukraine my father, Leanid Nossov, was taken away in the middle of the night never to be heard from again. During that time, the people of Kiev were afraid to go to bed at night. They feared that dreaded knock on their door. But many families did hear that fateful sound and they had to deal with it and suffer just as our family did.

Many months after Father's disappearance, a close friend of his appeared on our doorstep in the dark of the night. With a finger to his lips, he handed my mother Father's gold ring and then he left in silence. That was how we learned that the Communists had executed my father. Father's only crime was his education and the possession of family wealth. Because of this, Leanid Nossov was branded as an enemy of the people. After that, we were shunned by our close friends and neighbors. They feared that any association with us also would mark them as an enemy of the state. Everyone feared for their lives.

Grandmother had a younger sister, Ulyana, who lived not far from them in Kiev. She often came to visit us on Sundays. Even though they were sisters, the two women looked quite different in many respects. Grandmother was small and demure, while Aunt Ulyana was tall and willowy. Grandmother had auburn-red hair while Aunt Ulyana had strawberry-blonde hair. Still it was easy to tell they were sisters; their likeness was stamped on their faces and was shown in their charming family mannerisms.

When the two sisters were together, Grandfather called them, "my two redheads." I never heard much about my grandparents' courtship but Grandfather often called Grandmother, "my petite redhead." I remember them as old people but, even then, it was easy to see that there was a deep and abiding love between them.

Mother and Me

I remember well the late spring and early summer of 1941. I was still basking in the sunshine of comparative peace and happiness in the home of my grandparents even as World War II raged all around us. Their home was located on the outskirts of Kiev—equivalent to an American suburb. Their neighborhood was close to public transportation which made it fast and easy for Mother to come and go as she needed.

My mother worked in the Kiev school system; all women were required to work in Communist society whether they were married, single or mothers with children. Mother had a small apartment in a six-story cement building in downtown Kiev. Our belongings were divided between our two homes. During the week, before I started school, I lived weekdays with my wonderful grandparents but on most weekends, I lived with my mother unless she had a date or had to be out of town.

Mother took good care of me but she was not a

loving or caring parent to me. She often was critical of me and would never comfort me when I fell or hurt myself. Instead, she would severely scold me for being clumsy, yank me up and walk away. She broke my heart many times by telling me that I was ugly and stupid. She said my ugly nose always dripped like a faucet. She especially hated my blonde eyebrows.

I remember how, with envy, I saw other mothers hug and kiss their children but my mother hardly ever hugged me. Once I asked my mother if I could kiss her on the cheek. I never will forget how, reluctantly, she leaned down towards me with a frightful grimace on her face and allowed me to kiss her. She did not kiss me in return.

My grandparents were everything to me that my mother was not. They loved me unconditionally. Even though nothing was ever said about Mother's behavior towards me, I knew that they understood and felt badly about it.

When I was with my grandparents, I felt loved, cared for and safe. I was their first grandchild and a joy in their old age. Even though, at times, I was a handful, I was never intentionally naughty because I loved them with all my heart. Often, my dear grandparents praised me for my good behavior and covered my face with kisses as a reward.

Grandmother often said, "You are a good helper for a girl your age." She was right. I loved to work in the kitchen with her because she made work seem more like fun. And Grandfather often said, "You are the sunshine of my old age." Our bond of love grew as time went on and only became stronger and closer during the most difficult times.

Grandfather and Me

I remember how proud I was of my grandfather. He was a medical doctor—an ear, nose and throat specialist. Everyone loved and respected him. Grandmother was first of all a loving wife, a good cook, a great homemaker and the best Grandmother in the world. She loved me but she was very strict. Grandmother ruled the house while Grandfather ruled our lives. In other words, Grandmother was in charge of all the everyday things like sewing, cooking and cleaning, while Grandfather took charge of the big things like doctoring, finances and politics.

Shortly before World War II broke out, Grandfather was forced to retire at the early age of sixty-five. All his friends and family said, "He still is a young man." To me he looked pretty old, but now, in my seventies, I know what they meant. It was a shame because Grandfather was still full of vitality with mental and physical energy to spare. According to the retirement policies of the Communist regime it was time for him to step down and make room for the next generation of young doctors.

After his retirement, Grandfather felt lost with nothing to do and nothing to look forward to. He was a man who had dedicated his entire life to the medical profession and his family. He still had his family but now had no other interests. Grandmother was a dedicated homemaker and a good wife but she was too busy running the house to have much time for silly events like movies, opera or ballet. So I became my grandfather's best pal and companion.

Often, on Saturday afternoon, we went to the opera; Saturday afternoon performances were free, compliments of the Communist Party. I loved Bizet's *Carmen* but most other operas were too long, too boring and too difficult for me to understand. In that case, I would curl up in the seat next to Grandfather, snuggle up close to him and fall asleep. On the way home after the performance, Grandfather would sing his favorite arias in his best deep voice with the silliest gestures to explain the meaning of Italian lyrics to me. I loved to hear him sing. Those were very happy days for me.

On alternate Saturday afternoons, we went to the ballet, that I loved. On the way home, it was my turn to do the jumps, leaps and pirouettes mimicking the routines of the great dancers. Together, Grandfather and I had great fun! Quite often, he told me, "Acting silly with you makes me feel young again." I understand now what he meant.

My Dreams of Grandeur

I remember the day I turned seven years old on March 15, 1941. As long as I could remember, I had big dreams of becoming a famous Prima Ballerina. In the mornings, as soon as I woke up, I would roll over on my back, extend my legs into the air and point my toes toward the ceiling, pretending I already was a great ballerina! I admired my legs, my arched foot and my strong ankles, essential attributes for a ballerina. I envisioned my legs as long and slender. My strong ankles looked beautiful to me. In truth, my legs were too skinny and my knee joints were larger than my thighs. As a child, I was an extremely finicky eater and my grandmother worried I would grow up to be a midget or would starve myself to death.

In the summer of 1941, my ambition to become a dancer drove me to walk with my feet turned out as if they were locked in first position permanently. I must have looked more like Charlie Chaplin than a ballerina—feet turned to the outside as I waddled from side to side. Thinking back, it is obvious that I was very conscious of my body, my posture and my manner of walking.

When I sat on a chair or a sofa, I would sit tall and straight with my legs crossed at the ankles, as a young lady should. I held my hands in a limp and graceful position with the thumbs and pinkies almost touching like dancers do. I held my back straight with my neck stretching tall, as if my head was reaching to the ceiling. I heard my grandmother often say, "You have to suffer to be beautiful." I was willing to suffer; suffering sounded so glamorous to me at that time. That was before I endured war.

Grandmother told me, "Spanish teenage girls wore Mandarin collars starched and ironed to a razor-sharp edge. If they let their head droop the slightest they could get a nasty cut on their chin or throat. That is how the Spanish girls were trained to have graceful swan-like necks."

My grandmother was full of these old sayings and all I had to do was hear them once or twice and they would become my own ideas.

I had long blonde hair that reached almost to my waist but I thought my hair was not long enough. I would bend my head backwards until my head touched my shoulder blades making my hair long enough to almost reach my buttocks. Only then would I be satisfied. Besides, early on, I realized that bending my head backwards also stretched my neck. That way I killed two birds with one stone.

Like most young girls, I loved new clothes. Since I was the only granddaughter, my grandmother made many pretty dresses for me. But hard as I tried, I could never convince her to let me wear more than one clean dress in a day unless we were going somewhere special or had company coming to visit us. That seemed unreasonable to me but I could not change her mind. Grandmother was a smart lady. She knew I could soil several dresses in one day if she let me. That would mean more clothes to wash. In 1941, automatic washing machines were unheard of in Kiev, Ukraine.

I was a creative child and when I soiled my dress while eating bread with jam or playing in the mud, I would turn the dress so the dirty front would become the back and the clean back would become the front. I would smile to myself and think that it was the same as having two dresses in one day.

Going to Church with Grandfather

I remember Sunday mornings when, hand-in-hand, Grandfather and I walked to the Greek Orthodox Church nearest to our home; even though, officially, it was the Russian Orthodox Church, in our family we called it the Greek Orthodox Church. I loved going to church; I got to wear my pretty dress with new shoes and socks to match. Grandmother always reminded me, "Don't forget your little bag with a handkerchief and money for the church." Even though Grandmother was a religious person, she never went to church with us on Sunday. But she never missed the all-night Easter service.

We usually arrived early on Sunday morning so that Grandfather could visit with his old pals and show me off. With a twinkle in their eyes, his old cronies would say, "What a pretty girlfriend you have here."

Grandfather would sternly correct them, "She is not my girlfriend; Lorissa is my seven-year-old granddaughter."

Another old friend would say, "She is too small and delicate for her age."

That was music to my ears since I always wanted to be petite. Grandmother often said, "A fine lady should be small and delicate."

Then finally, grandfather would say, "She is not too small for seven; besides, all good things come in small gift baskets."

At church, along with the good, I had to accept

the bad. We always were offered Communion on Sunday—that was the good part. Then, after the service, we walked home and grandfather always warned me not to spit. He said sternly, "You just received Holy Communion, your spit is holy, don't let it fall on the dirty ground."

According to Grandfather, to spit out any crumb of Holy Communion was a sin worse than death—that was the bad part. The minute my grandfather said that, saliva appeared in my mouth seemingly out of nowhere and I began to drown in my own juices. Not until we arrived home to the good smells of Sunday dinner did I forget all about spitting.

Grandmother was a wonderful cook. I loved her strawberry jam the best! She made many other delicious traditional Ukrainian dishes. The main meal of the day was usually served in three courses. On Sundays, everyone was expected to be dressed nicely for dinner. Every European nation has its own national vegetable soup and Borscht is the Ukrainian/Russian national soup. Borscht and black bread was and still is the mainstay of the Ukrainian diet. At a Sunday dinner, Borscht is served as the first course with a dollop of sour cream in the center of each soup plate. The first course is followed by meat, vegetables and potatoes or pasta and rice. Sometimes meat-stuffed vareniki were served with salads as second course; vareniki are similar in taste and texture to Chinese pot stickers.

Dessert and tea was my favorite part of the meal. Always, Grandmother used her best china on Sundays. The tea was served in fine china cups with saucers. It was a sin, according to Grandmother, to use a cup without a saucer. Ceramic mugs were unheard of in Grandmother's home. Tin mugs were used by blue-collar workers to drink water on the job and sometimes at home. Small-sized tin cups hung on a chain from a cold water bucket at the bazaars and other public places. Water was sold for one kopek a cup.

We gathered around the samovar, a traditional antique-silver tea maker, to finish our meal with a dessert, usually cake or a tort or fruit and cheeses with hot tea. This was my favorite part of the meal.

Grandmother also made great perozhki. These are pastries filled with well-seasoned ground meat and vegetables. Then the perozhki were either baked in the oven or deep-fried in oil. Perozhki are the Ukrainian version of America's famous hamburgers. Venders sell perozhki warm in Kiev at most public gatherings such as parades, bazaars or sports events. They are tasty, nutritious and easy to eat on the go, just like hamburgers.

3. The War Comes to Kiev

By the summer's end in 1941, no longer was everything fun and games, even for me. These were now serious and dangerous times in our home and in our land. Late in the evening, old friends and neighbors gathered to visit my grandparents while I was supposed to be asleep, but I could not sleep. In the quiet of the night, I heard their anxious whispers about war and their fearful sighs.

Whenever the conflict between Germany and Russia was even slightly mentioned, I could taste fear. I really had no idea what the elders were talking about but I was scared! Many times they would stop talking when I slid down the banister into the living room. Instead of laughter and clapping as it had been in days gone by, they stared at me with their fearful eyes full of the knowledge of what was yet to come and I would disappear behind the doors of my bedroom. At times like that, the silence of my grandparents and their friends was too oppressive for me to bear. Yet, in the late summer of 1941, World War II still seemed far away. In spite of my fears, I felt safe, happy and blessed.

My Education Is Terminated

In the fall of 1941, I was a second grader in a two-story gray cement school building located in downtown Kiev, not far from the apartment house where Mother and I lived. I walked to and from school past the old Taras Schevchenko Park. At the entrance to the park there stood a statue of this famous Ukrainian poet and philosopher, who stood with outstretched arms near the gate as if to welcome all who came.

As the students entered the school building, the first room they came to was a long, wide hall with the lower half of the walls painted shiny-bright green, while the upper half of the walls and the ceiling were painted dull white. My second grade classroom was on the second floor along with the third and fourth grade classrooms. The first grade students and preschoolers were on the first floor as was the lunchroom and the library. Every morning, I ascended the hardwood steps of the worn-out staircase with a banister that was so high I could barely hook my chin over the massive wooden handrail. Waiting in my large classroom was a pretty young teacher to educate us.

One day, as I was standing at the top of the stairs, a horde of children spilled out past me from one of the other classrooms. They were running and yelling, "The Germans are coming! The Germans are coming!"

The teachers were yelling too, "Hurry home! Go home! Hurry! Hurry!"

The teachers said, "Tell your parents that the school will be closed until war is over."

I was scared. The scene of panic gave me a sick feeling in the pit of my stomach, as if a huge iron hand was squeezing the life out of me. The same kind of fear was squeezing the life out of the adults, including my dear grandparents. From that day on, whenever I saw shiny green walls, I was reminded of pain, panic and chaos. That was the day my future, as I had believed it to be, came to an end.

That day, along with my education, my dance classes also were terminated, ending all my hopes and dreams of becoming a ballerina. In our school, all girls were required to take dance class in the first grade. By second grade, only the girls who made the cut could take dance classes. I had been fiercely proud to tell my grandparents that I was one of these girls. But now, it no longer mattered because there would be no more dance classes!

On this day, World War II became a reality to me; it was no longer just cautious whispers, sad looks and agonizing fear on people's faces.

The Bombing

One evening, shortly after the school was disbanded, my mother appeared, seemingly out of nowhere. After a short whispered conversation with my grandparents, she took me home to our flat in downtown Kiev. We were preparing to move in with my grandparents the next day and that evening and part of the night, we had to pack.

Later, on that night, I was awakened by an ear-piercing noise. The air raid sirens were wailing through the dark. The electricity was cut off from most of the homes in Kiev including ours. I pulled the covers tightly over my head as if to hide from the impending doom.

Then, Mother was shaking me, "Lorissa, wake up; quickly, get dressed. Hurry up!"

Even though I heard the urgency in her voice, I was so sleepy I could hardly keep my eyes open. At first, I heard the building pulsating as if a swarm of bees was circling us. Then the vibrations intensified and the building began to throb as if with a bad toothache.

Mother explained, "It is the German Blitzkrieg (air attack). They are trying to bomb Kiev into submission."

We ran out into the hall where we found that the two elevators were without electricity and were not working. We ran outside onto a wide cement catwalk that led to the fourth floor of another building. There we met a group of angry people returning from the basement bomb shelter. They told us that the bomb shelter was filled to capacity and the doors had been bolted shut from the inside. They were bitter. With profanity they railed against the Nazis for bombing us and against the Soviet government for not providing adequate bomb shelters for all of its citizens. We remained on the catwalk because we had nowhere else to go.

Mother was livid with me because I had not woken up when she called me. She insisted that if I had gotten up when she called, we might now be safe inside the bomb shelter.

Then we heard a group of men talking. Their anger had cooled and they said, "It is better to stay here and be killed outright than to be buried alive under tons of debris in the shelter." Mother felt better after she heard that.

That night I came face to face with my mortality. I understood that though I was not yet eight years old, my life could end at any moment.

The night was cold and clear. I could see the full moon, the twinkling stars, and the bombers flying in and out of the small white clouds. The city of Kiev was in total blackout but the full moon illuminated the buildings and the trees with an eerie silvery glow. We saw countless flashes of bright light which was the anti-aircraft artillery trying to bring down the bombers. Over and over again, the bombs fell all around us with thunderous explosions. Soon, I saw flames both close by and in the distance. We could smell the smoke from burning buildings and we could hear voices crying for help. Without being told, I knew that we could be next at any moment. This was the most terrifying night of my young life.

My insides were being gripped with anxiety. I wanted to run, to get away from this horrible place but we were all trapped and could not move.

Many people around us were praying out loud with their hands folded close to their faces as they looked up to the sky. These people were the citizens of an atheistic society. They were biblically illiterate and yet, they were looking to God for deliverance. Others were screaming at the top of their lungs for help, directed to no one in particular.

That night, I saw grown men crying like children, with tears streaming down their faces. Until that day, I had not known that men cried. A young woman standing next to us was holding a tiny infant in her arms. She told Mother how anxious she felt for her baby. Then she said, "I need to be brave for my husband's sake; he is somewhere on the front lines."

She buried her face in her baby's blue blanket while the bombs were falling all around us like snowballs. I watched her sobbing. Her whole body shook. Then, I noticed a puddle forming at her feet; a thin veil of steam rose into the cold air but, consumed by grief, she was not aware of it.

Next to us on the other side, a middle-aged woman lay on the floor rolled up into a fetal position. She was whimpering like a child. Her silhouette looked slight and strangely pathetic in the moonlight.

Through all this tragedy, Mother was unnaturally silent. She just held me tightly as if to shield me from harm.

And I? I did not cry. I did not pray. I did not talk. With my eyes wide open, I saw and internalized everything that was happening around me. To this day, I remember that night and I can still see the people. I was hurting for everyone I saw but especially for my mother. In the dark of that night, my deepest fears rose to the surface—I wanted to live.

From fright, my insides began churning and cramping again. Suddenly, without a warning, vomit burst forth violently from my mouth like a volcano erupting, spraying everything within close range.

Mother exploded with anger at me. Not only had I soiled the front of my dress but I also had covered Mother's skirt, her legs and her shoes with vomit.

Everyone reacts differently to stressful circumstances. Vomiting was a painful catharsis for me while anger was an outlet for my mother, a release from the horrors of that night.

When I woke up in the morning back in our apartment, the sun was already up. Mother was busy packing. She said, "Wake up! We were lucky last night but if we stay here, we might not be as lucky the next time."

By the end of that day, and with the help of our friends, we were all moved into my grandparents' home. We knew we would be much safer there with them.

The second time the Germans bombed Kiev, we were safely tucked away in my grandparents' home. The damage done to the heart of Kiev that night was listed on the front page of the newspaper. Among the buildings totally destroyed was our apartment complex. The article simply stated that the six-story building had been destroyed along with all the people who were in the bomb shelter. They had all perished!

It was plain to see that the Germans were bombing mostly the government centers located in downtown Kiev and the industrial complexes located on the northeastern side of the city. They were not interested in quiet residential areas and that was lucky for us.

The Invasion

I remember how several weeks after the air raid the invasion of Kiev began in earnest with heavy artillery fire from both sides. One sunny morning, I was playing on the floor in front of my little stool serving tea to my dolls. I heard a loud 'swisssh' going over our house. Then, there was a powerful explosion in the distance. Everything in the house rattled and shook, including my toy dishes. It felt like an earthquake!

Grandfather said, "This is bad! We are in the line of fire. Let us all pray to God for protection and go to the root cellar as quickly as possible."

From Grandfather's tone of voice, I knew we were in great danger. That first rocket was only one of many more to come. Some came during that night, even more next morning and many more in the following days. It was a three-day siege that seemed to last a lifetime.

The German army was attacking from the south-eastern side of Kiev. The Russians were defending from the northwestern side. The Nazis were firing heavy artillery shells and rockets over the city and over the heads of the defenseless citizens. The Russians were answering in kind and the people of Kiev were caught in the middle. We were never warned, nor did we have a chance to evacuate. The Soviets were too busy fighting the Germans, while the Ukrainians were just an expendable commodity in the deadly game of war.

After the artillery exchange stopped, we did not see any hand-to-hand street combat in our neighborhood. There was only a deadly silence! The stillness was more frightening than the thunder of artillery. To us, anything would have been better then that eerie silence. No one knew what was happening. We had no radio or any other communication. Not until we saw the Red Army's ragtag soldiers running through our kitchen garden and jumping over the fence did we realize that the Nazis were now in charge.

I heard Grandfather ask, "Is Kurenevka District (where we lived) on our side or on the enemy side?" But there was nobody who knew the answer to his question.

During the siege of Kiev, my grandparents ordered me to stay in the house. Then, in the afternoon on September 17, 1941, my grandmother rushed breathlessly into my room, grabbed me by the hand and said, "Let's go to the park to see the Germans." The park, Petropavlvovskaya Square, was not far from our home. I tried to tell Grandmother that I did not have my shoes on, only my socks. But she replied, "It is all right. Today is a warm and sunny day. Be happy. The battle is over! It is good to be alive!!"

In the middle of the Square, a large group of German soldiers was resting on the grass, leaning against their huge tanks and cannons. Ukrainian people, young and old, (all middle-aged men and women were on the front lines fighting the Nazis) encircled the soldiers three and four bodies deep. I pushed to the front, dragging Grandmother with me. There I saw blond-haired, rosy-cheeked young German soldiers and their commanders. Their gray-green uniforms were battle-worn and dusty but the soldiers looked well-dressed and well-fed. In comparison, the Soviet soldiers looked like beggars. They wore ragged, ill-fitting and mismatched uniforms with worn-out boots. Good boots meant life itself for the soldiers; worn-out boots meant certain death during winter in Ukraine or Russia. All Soviet soldiers had hollow eyes and a 'lean and hungry look,' as described by Shakespeare in "Julius Caesar."

While they were resting, most of the Nazi soldiers cradled their rifles in their arms like a mother holding her baby. They were ready for anything at any moment. The crowd was hushed. With wide-open eyes, the Ukrainian people stared at their invaders as if they were looking at gods.

Many Ukrainian people, including my grandparents, hoped against all hope that the German Army would liberate them from the many decades of Communist oppression.

This was not to be. The Nazis were even worse tyrants than the Communists. If the Nazis had proven to be our liberators, most of the Ukrainian people would have been ready to stand on their side. In such an event, the outcome of World War II might have been quite different. But the Nazis had a different agenda; they were out to promote the Aryan Race and determined to destroy anyone who did not fit that mold.

Mother's Secret Life

Late one night, a few days after the Germans occupied Kiev and things began to settle down a bit, my mother returned from one of her many mysterious missions. I was asleep but when I heard the low whispers, I recognized my mother's voice. At the time, I was too young to understand all that went on around me but I knew it was unnatural to hear low voices and unfinished sentences. It hurt me to see the worried looks and tears of my grandparents but it seemed to me that our troubles were over since my mother was now home.

Little by little, I learned from my grandparents some things about my mother. Mother was a bright young lady with some higher education, which was rare for women in those days. She was multi-lingual, able to speak Russian, Ukrainian, Polish and some German. These assets turned out to be a heavy burden for her. She was singled out and forced against her will to become an undercover courier for the Soviets.

Mother traveled to many parts of the Soviet Union occupied by the Germans to make contacts with other agents and to exchange military secrets. She carried secret documents across borders and completed dangerous assignments, knowing she could be caught and shot at any time. Mother was never told who her allies or her enemies were until the last moment when the contact was made. She was warned that if she did not cooperate, something dreadful would happen to her, her only child and her aged parents.

This new-found knowledge answered many of my questions: Why was mother gone so much? Who were the high-ranking Soviet military men who appeared at our door and whisked her away? Why did she have to go with them when she had just arrived home?

To this day, many details about my mother's secret life still are not clear to me and never will be. During War World II, Mother endured many hardships of which I had very little knowledge at the time. Many forces converged to break her down: the stress of war, the fear associated with being an undercover courier, the deadly fear of the Germans, the submission to Communist blackmail, and the heavy responsibilities of being a single parent. These many pressures resulted in Mother experiencing a serious nervous breakdown in later years which left her unable to cope with the realities of life in general and with her children in particular.

As she grew older, Mother became suspicious of everyone and everything and eventually she turned on those who loved her.

She was unable to open up to anyone including her daughter, Lorissa, and her son, Edward.

In time, she explained a little why she was so short-tempered with me. She regretted all the time she had to spend away from me. She regretted being unable to give me love and comfort when I needed it. One thing she said over and over again, "My mind was filled with fear and danger; there was no room for anything else."

Mother took many of her secrets with her to her grave. Even though I do not know all the details about her past, I know she was in great peril during the war years and that she did it all for her family.

4. The Enemy Lurks among Us

I remember how in the first week of occupation, the German army was visible everywhere and, to the Ukrainians, they seemed harmless. An uneasy peace settled between the Ukrainian people and the Germans. The Nazis were busy looking for suitable buildings to occupy as their permanent headquarters. In the end, public school buildings were their choice since many departments could be housed in one large complex. The Nazis also were becoming acquainted with the layout of the city. At the same time, they were trying to impress and frighten the Ukrainian people with their fierce show of might and power.

They drove in long lines as if on parade, showing off their tanks, their trucks loaded with Nazi soldiers, other trucks loaded with supplies and more pulling cannons. The main parade was followed by smaller official vehicles packed with smiling officers, waving to the Ukrainian people as if to say, "We are the conquerors!" These were alarming shows of force.

During the occupation, the people of Kiev suffered many shortages. All sorts of public services were cut off. There was a total disruption of public transportation. Hospital doors were closed and medical personnel was evacuated along with the Red Army to the war front. Most, if not all, grocery stores were looted and stood empty. All local radio stations were disrupted, causing a total blackout of information in Kiev.

Poor Grandfather, he missed his daily newspaper the most. His face was grave when he found out that the newspapers had been canceled for an indefinite period. Instead of the morning paper, we were directed to read the one-page leaflets produced by the Nazi regime and crudely nailed to the walls of the empty public buildings and on fences along well-traveled streets and roads.

The leaflets were one-sentence directives: "All curfews must be strictly obeyed. Anyone caught on the streets between dusk and dawn will be shot and their dead bodies will be hung from the lampposts as an example to all the people."

At night, young hooligans, like wolves, roamed the streets in packs. They were looting and destroying Kiev. The young plunderers were not looking for luxury items like jewelry and art, which were useless. Food was more valuable to them than gold and they were looking for bread and potatoes. But these thugs did not understand that by looting Ukraine, they were destroying themselves. Soon the news was out that the looters were being caught and killed in large numbers by the Nazis.

Sometimes, after dark, when we were slowly slipping into an uneasy sleep, we were awakened by the sound of heavy Nazi boots pounding on the cement sidewalk outside our house. Then we would hear a loud command, "Halt! Halt!" Often, shots rang out, followed by a cry of pain. Other times, we heard a feminine voice cry for help but no one was able to come to the aid of those poor women.

It was not safe for teenage girls or young women to be out on the streets, day or night. Many defense-less females were abducted and locked up in holding pens by German soldiers. These unfortunate young women first were raped by countless Nazi officers, then gang-raped by soldiers and finally killed.

At first, when the weather was still nice, Grand-mother went to the open-air market instead of Mother or me to trade for food and wood. But when the weather turned cold and the snow was getting deep, it became more difficult for Grandmother to walk a long distance by herself and to carry heavy bundles.

On the following week, Grandfather directed Mother to dress like an old woman with a hump on her back. She smeared soot to make black circles under her eyes, smudged dirt on her face and blackened her teeth with paint. With a heavy scarf on her head, Mother looked like a Russian Babushka. She looked ugly enough to be unattractive to Nazi soldiers or anyone else. In this way, she was able to go out to trade for food and fuel. Since the occupation, I had not been allowed to go out. I understood and bore my imprisonment bravely but I missed walking on the frozen snow that crunched under my feet and throwing a snowball or two at my mother.

The first time Mother went out dressed like a hag, she looked too ugly for words and we laughed with her. But when she returned from the bazaar, she had a surprise for us. Mother said, "When I arrived at the market, there were many other hunchbacked ugly women dressed just like me."

Grandfather said, "I am glad that other families had the presence of mind to protect their young women and girls."

Finding Food, Water, Fuel

I remember how during the long summer and fall of 1941, Grandmother gathered and stashed away a lot of dry food that would keep well for a long period of time, things like dry beans, barley grain, flour, sugar, dry peas, potatoes, carrots, onions, cabbages and sauerkraut salted down in large wooden barrels. We hung homemade noodles, cookies and sliced dried bread from the ceiling. I helped to slice, dry and bag the foods that would save our lives later on.

But fuel was hard to get and we knew the harsh winter was coming. Every bit of wood we bought, traded for or found was hidden in the basement, under beds, under tables and other out-of-the-way places. In the pre-war days, Grandfather used to order a load of wood and a load of coal delivered to our house. This amount of fuel kept us warm and comfortable all winter long.

After the Nazi occupation, this service was no longer available. Lack of hay and grain caused desperate farmers to kill their horses and sell them for meat. That did away with all delivery services. People had to walk everywhere and one person could not carry much fuel either on his back or in her arms, even if the fuel was available.

Walking made us more vulnerable. Every time we stepped outside our home, we were in mortal danger. The Nazis liked it that way because we were visible and accessible to them. Not a day went by that we did not hear shots ringing out close by. We knew that with every shot, someone had died at the hands of the Nazis.

Before dawn and after dusk, Grandfather brought in armloads of wood from the kitchen garden (in Ukraine, flowers are grown in the front of the house while the vegetables are raised in the kitchen garden in the back yard). Grandfather was quietly dismantling our back yard fence in the dark so that neighbors and passing strangers would not notice what he was up to.

One morning, when Grandfather went out to bring in more wood, he found that the rest of the fence was gone! The wooden barrels, wooden benches and other things made of wood also were gone. That was the end of our private stash of wood. Grandfather was heartbroken. He blamed himself for not getting the wood in sooner. He kept saying, "The thugs stole the rest of the fence in one night. Why didn't we hear or see them last night? It takes a long time to take down half a fence, I know. There must have been three or more husky men working hard last night."

Living during wartime is a dog-eat-dog existence; if you don't get there first, the dogs will. It did not matter to whom the items belonged; overnight, they were stolen.

Grandfather's Illness

By early winter, Grandfather was not feeling well. He tried to put on a brave face and deny any signs of illness. But his tall, thin body gave him away. When he stood up, he swayed like a willow tree in the wind. His face had a gray pallor and his eyes were deeply sunken. He hardly ate and he was always cold. My job was to bring him hot-water bottles for his feet and hands. I loved my grandfather dearly. I would have done anything to help him. It brings tears to my eyes as I remember.

Grandfather never complained. Instead, he was always cheerful just to keep our spirits up. During the day, he refused to rest. He continued to be useful by chopping wood for kindling and all the while telling us stories about the past that kept us from thinking about the present and our miserable existence.

One day, unexpectedly, an old friend of our family, a retired doctor, came to visit us. Later we found out that Grandmother secretly had asked the doctor to help us. After a modest lunch and a pleasant conversation, the doctor gave Grandfather a thorough examination. After it was over, Grandfather said to the doctor, "Do not go behind a closed door and talk about my condition. Tell us here and now about your diagnoses. We all need to know."

The doctor sat down next to Grandfather and took his hand. We all, Mother, Grandmother and I, were dying on the inside for fear of what the doctor had to say.

In short and concise sentences, he told us that Grandfather's heart was wearing out fast. The stress of war, worry for his family's safety and the lack of adequate nourishment were the main causes for his ill health.

The doctor assured Grandmother, "What you are doing for Vasil is the best, under these difficult circumstances. You are a brave woman. God bless you!"

I was surprised to hear God's name used in this way. Usually, I heard God's name used only in vain.

After the doctor's visit, Grandfather regained his strength for a while. He wanted to help us in any way he could but his best help was advising us; his mind was still young and sharp.

Grandfather said, "I feel it in my bones, this will be a bitter winter. There will be three or more months of freezing weather. I am afraid our wood supply will run out long before spring arrives. We need to close off the two bedrooms upstairs and the living room downstairs to conserve fuel. We will use the kitchen for cooking, heating and eating and we will sleep in the adjoining dining room by night and use it as a living room by day. We will have to go through the cold bedroom to use the bathroom but that is the best we can do."

Grandfather's suggestions set off a frenzy of activity. That day, for the first time in many days, everyone was warm. In fact, we were hot! Instead of worrying about our troubles or listening for Nazi soldiers who might break through our door, we were happy being busy. I thought moving and pulling and tugging our belongings was great fun. Just the thought of sleeping in the same room with my grandparents was more than I could stand. It was pure excitement for me!

We moved two big beds into the dining room—one bed for my grandparents and the other for Mother and me. Then we moved in two big mattresses, bedding, pillows and every quilt and blanket we could find. When I thought we were done, we still had to move all that stashed wood and hide it again under our beds and in other safe places.

Grandfather's Priceless Legacy
I remember that after we moved into the din-

ing room, the many nights that followed were most delightful. Grandfather was an amazing storyteller. He made us forget the dreadful war that was raging all around us. His powers of observation were formidable and his memory was that of a young man. He remembered everything to the slightest detail. For women, he never neglected to mention pretty dresses or colorful flowers. And for the men, he always described hunting or fishing with the most exciting details—it was like lights, camera and action! When he talked about food, I could almost taste it. When he talked about performances, I could visualize them and I would be transported there.

Grandfather never hurried; his voice was soft, his delivery was slow and deliberate, but he was never boring. He enjoyed sharing and he savored the memories of the past days of his youth. But above all, Grandfather was factual to the smallest detail; no matter how bizarre his story seemed, we unquestioningly believed him. Grandfather was so careful to explain everything in detail; it was as if he sensed that soon we would part from each other and be gone from Kiev forever.

I was, after all, my grandfather's granddaughter and his legacy became my own talent. I internalized all that he ever said and it became my personal and priceless inheritance.

Most of the time, we went to bed early because there was no electricity and candles had to be carefully saved for emergencies. We went to bed at dusk to keep warm and to listen to Grandfather's stories of his youthful exploits. It was the most wonderful escape for me during those long, scary black nights.

As my grandfather relived his experiences, I saw him in my mind as a handsome young medical student. He was fortunate to be from a well-to-do family who sent him to Austria to study at the University of Vienna. He had to work harder than most of his Austrian classmates since he had to learn the Austrian language as well as study medicine. He was a good student and always received high grades.

As a medical student, Grandfather was inducted into the Tsar's Army during World War I (1914–1918). He became a medical officer who followed his assigned unit into battle. After each battle, he treated scores of wounded men and saw horrific suffering. Grandfather often said, "Those who died were the lucky ones!"

I was always eager to hear my favorite story about the five hungry wolves: One day, while working with the wounded soldiers, a high-ranking doctor ordered Grandfather to ride his horse over to the next village for medical supplies. He started out right after lunch.

Grandfather was unfamiliar with the region but he had been given good directions to follow. Soon, however, he was lost. While he was retracing his tracks, the daylight turned to dusk and then dark. Grandfather knew it was not wise to bed down in the open field and there were no villages close by as far as he could see.

He sensed the presence of wolves close by. He knew he had to save himself and his horse. So he unsaddled his horse and removed its bridle, slapped the animal on the rump and yelled, GO! The horse took off at a fast gallop leaving Grandfather to deal with the wolves.

There was no time to waste. The wolves were cautiously advancing in a tight pack. Nearby stood a good-sized evergreen tree and the decision was made for Grandfather. He stacked the horse tack and his belongings in a pile under the tree. He took out his sharp knife and cut himself, drawing enough blood to cover the knife blade. He wedged the handle of the knife tightly into the crotch of a tree, low enough for wolves to reach it. Then, quickly, Grandfather climbed up into the tree as high as its branches could support him.

It did not take long for the five wolves to smell the blood and surround the tree. They greedily licked the knife blade, thereby cutting their own tongues. In a feeding frenzy, the five hungry wolves fought among themselves to lick the knife until they were weak with the loss of their own blood.

In the morning, three of the wolves were gone but two of them lay dead not far from the tree. Three soldiers from his unit finally came looking for Grandfather, bringing his horse with them.

Another time, during a hasty retreat, there was much shooting and many loud battle cries. Grandfather's high-strung, fast-running horse got spooked and threw him off, causing Grandfather to slide on his face for many yards. The young medical officer now became a patient. After many months of convalescence, Grandfather recovered but his prominent slender nose was never straight again. From that day on, his nose slightly curved to the right side of his face. I can still remember gently tracing it with my fingertips whenever I sat on his lap.

Night after night, Grandfather poured his memories out to us. This was our inheritance, not the treasures of the world but memories of his wonderful Ukraine, of his beloved family and his interesting life. Grandfather left us a priceless legacy! The memories of those magic nights when we listened to him tell his stories in the dark have stayed with me a lifetime and will be passed on to my descendants.

Babi Yar

I remember how Grandfather often reminisced about his youthful days and about the home of his parents on the outskirts of Kiev. It was not far from the big ravine called Babi Yar (in Russian it means 'Witch's Gulch'). The ravine is still there and it is still huge even though it has undergone many horrific changes. During the Nazi occupation, a portion of the ravine closest to Kiev was filled with 33,000 murdered innocent souls.

In days gone by, superstitious people of Ukraine were afraid of the big ravine. Old women warned their grandchildren not to go near it. They said, "Evil spirits and witches roam Babi Yar looking for little boys and girls to eat."

Old and young men were fascinated by the huge ravine that sprawled over three districts, Kurenevka, Ludyanovka and Syrets Districts. (Ukraine is divided into districts as America is divided into states.) But most men and women were superstitious by nature and they stayed away from the big ravine.

At the bottom of the ravine ran a lively creek. In the spring, the creek boiled over rocks and boulders but in the fall, it meandered lazily over soft sand, collecting in a big, cool pool of water, only to spill over a rock-dam and continue on and on.

The dark abyss was overgrown with brambles and other clinging vines. Brave young souls picked blackberries, but only on the very edge of the ravine. Stinging nettles stood guard over the almost impassable trails that led to the bottom of the gulch.

Grandfather and his rascally pals spent many summer days in that deep gorge, hunting rabbits, fishing and swimming in those deep pools created by the creek.

As a child, I never saw the ravine, even though it was not far from our home in Kiev, but I listened well and remembered what Grandfather told me about the Great Gorge. Long ago, I promised myself that someday I would see Babi Yar with my own eyes.

In 1994 to 1996, I was a Peace Corps Volunteer in Hungary. In the summer of 1995, I was allowed to take a trip to the land of my birth, Kiev, Ukraine. I spent a whole day visiting and learning about Babi Yar. I was touched to the core of my being when I saw the three monuments dedicated to the Jewish people, the Ukrainian people and all the other people who had perished in the ravine.

But for the grace of God, I could have been one of those departed souls. The part of the ravine in the Kurenevka District was filled to the brim with the bodies of those who still cry out, "Remember us!"

In the olden days, no one talked much about the mysterious canyon. Its existence was almost unknown except to the people who lived close by. Babi Yar's infamy came about when the Nazis occupied Kiev. From the beginning, it was obvious that the Nazis knew all about Babi Yar's physical topography and they planned to use it for their cruel ethnic cleansing purposes.

During the occupation, the first wave of Nazi soldiers seemed almost benign compared to the second wave which seemed to be made up of bloodthirsty beasts. As days turned into weeks and fall became winter, the evil deeds of Nazism began to be exposed. As strangers, the Nazis had seemed harmless but through prolonged familiarity, contempt for the Nazis was born and grew in the hearts of the Ukrainian people.

Again, leaflets were hung on the walls of old buildings and on fences along the roads. The bold print demanded everyone's attention. With horror, people read and cried.

Attention All Jewish People!

In two days you must leave your home at seven o'clock in the morning and start walking.

The Nazi soldiers will guide you where you should go.

Two days after we read the leaflets, I woke up

to see my grandparents and Mother standing quietly at a parted curtain of a window. That was a strange sight for me. We had all agreed not to stand close to the window and, above all, never to part the curtains.

"We must not draw attention to ourselves," Grandfather sternly warned us many times.

I heard a strange little noise but I could not tell where it came from. It sounded like a helpless whimper. Then I saw my grandmother smothering her own sobs with her handkerchief held in her shaking hand. All three adults looked pale and alarmed.

I finally asked, "Can I see?" I stepped up on a stool and saw a river of human souls flowing past our house and on down our street. The Nazi soldiers were walking on both sides of the human column with bayonets mounted on their massive gray-green guns. Alongside the soldiers walked snarling German shepherd dogs with vicious teeth and foaming drool. The soldiers' guns were ready to be used on the poor, scared old people at any sign of provocation. The dogs, with hateful eyes, just like their masters, were willing to tear anyone apart at the first command. The column of humanity was marching shoulder-to-shoulder down the street that led to Babi Yar. I often wondered if they realized what awaited them at the end of the road. That morning, we did not know and it wasn't until later that we learned the tragic fate of these poor people.

As instructed by the Nazis, the Jewish people wore heavy coats. The men carried small suitcases filled with their valuables in one hand and a bag of food in the other. Some women carried a small tea kettle and a tiny bundle of dry wood. They looked and acted like slaves. They were totally submissive! They had lived a lifetime under an iron-fisted dictatorship of communism and they seemed to have lost their basic instinct for survival. There was no resistance in them.

I heard the rat-tat-tat, tat-tat, in the distance. To me, it sounded like the beating of the drums.

The Jewish people were directed to take off their shoes, coats and place their small suitcases on a large pile.

I heard the rat-tat-tat, tat-tat in the distance.

The victims were lined up shoulder to shoulder at the edge of the ravine, ready to fall in unison and to be swallowed up by the dark abyss of Babi Yar.

I heard the rat-tat-tat, tat-tat, in the distance.

The helpless souls fell broken and bleeding into the great canyon, one after another—again and again and again. . . .

I heard the rat-tat-tat, tat-tat, in the distance.

Another column of terrified martyrs was coming

to replace their fallen brothers and sisters.

I heard the rat-tat-tat, tat-tat, in the distance.

We wondered, "Are we going to be the next human sacrifices?"

All of us were helpless against the Nazi war machine. We watched from our windows in disbelief while the Jewish people continued to march quietly down the road. No one else became angry enough to stand up for our Jewish friends and neighbors. We all were afraid for our own lives!

A Small Act Of Resistance

I remember that several days after the exterminations had begun, in the middle of the night, we heard a faint knock on our back door. It was not a loud bang typical of the KGB or the Nazis. It was a timid knock. Mother went to the door with fear and trembling. It was our elderly little neighbor, Rosa. She, too, was trembling with fear. Quickly, Mother brought her into our dining room/bedroom. Rosa was crying and it took a while for her to control her emotions.

She said in a pleading voice, "Please, we need your help! My niece, who is half Jewish, has escaped from the great ravine."

We were shocked by this news. We knew what

would happen to us if we were caught helping our neighbor but we stood and listened to her story.

Rosa went on to say, "She fell with the rest of her family into the big gulch but somehow she was not touched by the Nazi gunfire. At first she was unconscious. When she came to, others were falling on top of her. She could not move because of the heavy weight of the dead bodies. Then she decided to just stay there until it was dark and all the soldiers were gone away for the night."

Rosa continued, "In the dark, she climbed over the countless dead bodies and out over the rim of the great ravine. She had no coat and no shoes. For fear of being seen, she crawled in the dark on all fours. When it was getting light she saw a huge haystack and used it to hide in. During the day, she had a chance to rest and get oriented. She heard Nazi trucks going by. That told her that the road to Kiev was close by. She was hungry, freezing—thank goodness it is still fall instead of winter—and hurt, but when it was dark, she continued to crawl and sometimes walk under the cover of darkness and hiding in the clumps of trees along the way. From crawling on all fours for many kilometers, her knees and hands are raw and bleeding."

Rosa went on to say, "She is hiding in my home right now. We need a coat, a dress and a pair of winter shoes for her so that she can continue her escape. Most in our family are small people but she is more Klaudia's size." My mother was a tall, big-boned woman while most Ukrainians are short and small-boned people.

We were never told the name of Rosa's niece but that night we were able to help that poor girl. Even though we never learned what happened to her, we hoped that she was successful in her attempt to escape.

Not long after that episode, Mother met Rosa on the street. They did not speak but our little neighbor winked and smiled at Mother. We felt it was a gesture of gratitude and a sign of success.

There were some partisan activities in the early months of occupation but they were too little too late. A few empty buildings were blown up but no serious harm was done to the Germans. The Nazis' response was swift and stern. Dozens of people, old women, children, and old men in that neighborhood were lined up on the street and shot. The dead were left lying where they fell for days as a reminder. A few days later, the Nazis came back to the same neighborhood demanding to know the names and whereabouts of the partisans. Nobody knew or would tell! Again, two dozen people were lined up and shot on the same spot. That discouraged the partisans from taking any more action.

When the Jewish people were forced to leave, they entrusted their house keys to their lifelong friends and close neighbors. Through their tears and with broken hearts, they pleaded with their friends to look after their homes and belongings. No sooner were the Jewish people out of sight, when their friends and neighbors greedily looted their homes. In some cases, they moved into the Jewish homes the very same day. My grandparents were outraged and were shocked at what was happening to their neighborhood.

With tears and a broken heart, Grandmother said, "In our time of need, there will be no one we can trust. We must cling to and depend on each other."

War makes selfish bullies out of otherwise kind and decent people. When poverty-stricken people are faced with temptation, they are often too weak to resist—not always for their own sake but often for the sake of their families. In many cases, they become guilt-ridden souls who question whether or not the world will ever forgive them and they hide their shame and guilt forever in silence.

Soon after the executions began, Babi Yar became a forbidden zone to all except the Nazis and those who were forced to work there covering the dead. The great ravine was ringed with high-voltage barbed wire and anyone who came near was shot on the spot.

In the second year of occupation, when the fortunes of war began to turn on the Nazis, thick smoke could be seen rising above the great gully for months. The air was filled with the acrid smell of burned flesh and diesel oil and a sprawling black cloud hovered over them like a funeral pall, smothering the people of Kiev.

I remember how Grandfather was deeply saddened when he heard how the Nazis had abused the playground of his youth. In days gone by Babi Yar was a place of happiness and joy to Grandfather and his boyhood friends. As small boys, they had run free and happy through the trees, where only their joyous laughter rang out to compete with the singing birds and the babbling brook. Now Babi Yar is a place of sadness, horror and death, not only for the Jewish people but also for Ukrainians, Russians, Gypsies and many others who would never see the same joy in Babi Yar as my grandfather and his pals saw.

5. Hardships of the Occupation

I remember how Grandfather continued to advise us from his easy-chair. He taught us how to manage our household and how to avoid harm during the most difficult time of our lives. He was too weak to do any physical work but his advice was invaluable. None of us realized how much Grandfather had done for us until he became physically unable to work.

One morning, before we were awake, Grandfather sat up in bed and said in panic, "Did anyone check the potatoes and carrots in the cellar lately?" Mother and Grandmother quickly got dressed and went to the cellar by the kitchen garden while I stayed with Grandfather to keep him company.

When Mother and Grandmother returned, their disappointment was written on their faces. By mid-November, earlier than usual, the weather had turned bitter cold and the vegetables were almost all ruined by the deep frost. That was a great blow to the plan for our survival. But we did salvage a bucket of frozen vegetables. Some of the carrots and cabbages were usable but the potatoes were beyond rescue. They were mushy with clear sap running out from under the skins.

By late November, we agreed to eat only two meals a day. On some days, we ate barley gruel with just a dab of butter in the mid-morning. And in late afternoon, we had one boiled potato each and a salted herring from the small wooden cask we had stashed away earlier. On other mornings, we had mush without milk but with two teaspoons of sugar and in the afternoon, we had meatless soup and a few slices of dry bread. Even though we were hungry, the frozen potatoes still tasted bad. We kept trying to eat them but they tasted icky-sweet and were awful-mushy but we did not suffer from food poisoning as some of our friends had predicted.

While having tea one afternoon, Mother and I noticed that Grandmother was drinking her tea without sugar. Mother asked her, "Why don't you use sugar? We all know you like it." But Grandmother shrugged her shoulders, put a finger to her lips and pointed to Grandfather. She was saving her sugar for her love. Mother followed Grandmother's example and from then on drank her tea straight. I tried to follow suit but the two older women strongly discouraged me.

We faced new challenges every day; one morning, we woke up to frozen water pipes in our house. The prolonged freezing weather and the unheated rooms had contributed to the problem. It was not just our home but the whole neighborhood had to deal with freezing weather. Even with gloves on, our fingers were so cold they did not work. Going to the bathroom was a big problem for us. We did not have zippers in those days and undoing buttons in a hurry with frozen fingers often caused me to have an accident. Trying to dry clothes in a freezing house was another big problem. It took two to three days to dry even lightweight articles of clothing.

Soon the word got around that there was running water a block up the street from us. Mother decided to go with a bucket to get some drinking water. I begged and pleaded with her to let me go but she would not agree to take me. Finally, Grandfather came to my aid and suggested that it would be safe for me to go. He knew a child needed exercise and it had been many weeks since I had been out of the house. It was a sheer delight to be out in the open air and snow. Yet, at the same time, it was scary. We all knew that at any moment, a Nazi soldier could step out from around a corner and mow us down with his machine gun.

The water was slowly trickling out of a half-frozen water pipe and the line of women with buckets was long. By the time all the women had filled their buckets and Mother had filled hers, an hour had passed. That gave me a chance to run and play with children my own age. When Mother got back home with water and me with rosy cheeks, my grandparents were overjoyed to see us safe and happy.

We had a family meeting about the scarcity of drinking water. Everybody had their say before we come up with a water saving plan. Grandfather said, "Klaudia is able to bring only enough water for cooking and to do dishes. Mother insisted, "I can bring an extra pail of water if needed."

A discussion about water conservation was initiated by Grandfather. He said, "Since water will be scarce until spring, and being out on the street to get water is not safe, we need a plan for how to conserve water."

A plan was conceived on how to use the same water three times. With a small amount of warm water, Mother and I were to brush our teeth, then wash up and then wash our underwear in the same bowl. Grandmother and Grandfather followed the same pattern with another bowl of water. The same plan was used in the kitchen; we used warm water to prepare food for cooking, then we washed the dishes, then the dish towels and then scrubbed the floors. This way, we made our water go a long way.

This plan worked well until it snowed. After many days of blizzard, the snow started to pile up high around our house, so high that it was up over our window sills. Mother had a bright idea. "Why don't we gather the snow into buckets and melt it by the stove in the kitchen. That will give us extra water to wash ourselves better and to wash some of our outer clothing. This will solve our problem until spring."

That sounded like a fun idea to me. Soon, however, it became a heavy chore for us. A handful of snow is not heavy but to carry a bucket full of packed snow was a backbreaking task.

Once again, new leaflets were posted. Mother took me with her to read the news. We saw people with dread on their faces crowding to read the leaflets but this time the news was good. It was announced that from then on, every citizen of Kiev would receive one loaf of bread once a week. Our neighborhood was directed to a nearby office building where each person would sign up to receive a packet of dated bread stamps. We were allotted only three packets since Grandfather was too ill to represent himself in person.

Ukrainian people are not stupid. We knew that

registering for bread stamps was a way for the Nazis to get information about Kiev's population but there was nothing we could do about it. We were captives in our own city in every sense of the word.

It was lucky for us that the bakery was close to our home so that Grandmother could register and get her bread. We came home with three loaves of black bread (Ukrainian black bread is baked in large, round, flat loaves). The bread smelled good and felt fresh but when we bit into it, we realized that there was something dreadfully wrong with the texture. The bread was rough, chewy and hard to swallow. It scratched our throats going down and made us cough persistently.

It did not take long for Grandmother to pin down the mysterious ingredient in our new bread. "They added sawdust to the bread," she said. We all agreed with her finding but we ate the bread anyway--sawdust and all. It was an acceptable addition to our thin meatless soup and, in a way, this bread made up for the loss of our potatoes.

Early one morning, Mother and I woke up to the sound of chopping and of Grandmother crying. In our nightgowns, we ran into the cold living room to see Grandfather chopping on their beautiful hardwood chiffonier while Grandmother, on her knees, was begging him to stop.

"This was our wedding present from my parents. Don't you remember? Please stop destroying our memories," pleaded Grandmother.

But Grandfather's mind was made up. He stopped chopping, took Grandmother into his arms and said, "I am sorry, my dear, but we need this wood to survive."

Grandmother understood and she stopped crying but she could not suppress her sobs. She continued to kneel on the cold floor watching Grandfather demolish her precious heirloom, rocking herself back and forth. It was so sad! Mother and I wept silently as we watched the old couple come to terms with their heartbreak.

As time went by, little by little, all hardwood furniture in the living room and in all other parts of the house, including the old grandfather clock, was chopped and burned. It took quite a bit of wood to start the coal burning.

The following Saturday morning Mother was on a mission. After the chopping of the chiffonier, she was determined to find some kind of fuel to put Grandfather's mind at ease. By mid-morning, she was dressed like an old woman and put Grandfather's heavy boots on. She put some bartering materials in a small bag, took my sled down from the wall and left for the bazaar all by herself.

6. Our Many Trips to the Bazaar

U kraine was a rich agricultural country, known all over the world as the Bread Basket of Europe. So what happened to all the farm produce? Thanks to Grandfather's patient teaching, I came to understand early in life what happened to the food that rightfully should have been ours.

Grandfather explained, "This is known as 'skimming the cream' system. First, the Soviet Army took all they could carry off from the big collective farms. Next, the Nazis had to feed their army. While fighting, they did not carry much of their own food with them but planned to commandeer whatever they needed from the countries they occupied. Both the Soviets and the Nazis took the best; the choicest beef, fattest pork, healthiest milk cows, the best wheat and potatoes, and the young chickens for meat and eggs. They cleaned out the Ukrainian storehouse so well that there was hardly anything left for the people of Kiev, not even milk for newborn babies and young children. From what they had left, the farmers had to feed themselves and their families before putting anything out on the market to feed the people of Kiev.

One Saturday morning, Mother and I, with my little sled, set out for the market. Mother was asking around for any coal that was available for sale when a man in his late forties, who was selling coal and wood, asked her, "Are you Klaudia Chomenko? Do you remember me?" Mother tried to remember but could not recall his name or place his face from her past.

Then the man told her, "I have been to your house many times. Your father doctored my son's serious ear infection many times several summers ago. He never charged me even one kopek (a Ukrainian kopek was like a U.S. penny). Your father knew I had no money but he never turned us away—God bless him."

The man, whose name was Ivan, said, "When I thanked your father, he always said, 'Someday, you will be able to help others. Do it cheerfully and from the kindness of your heart.'"

Ivan went on to say with a smile, "I have helped many people because of your father's kind example. He taught me to see and think with my heart and not just with my head. Today, I am able, in a small way, to repay my debt to your father. From now on, any day you come to the market, I will give you half a sack of coal."

When Mother told Grandfather the story, he bowed his head in silence as if remembering those days. Then he said with a faraway look in his eyes, "I remember Ivan, the young father with a sick boy in his arms, asking for help. He always arrived late in the evening. You see, Ivan worked long hard days on a collective farm. Tired and dirty, he carried his sick son many kilometers to my house. After the treatment, he still had to carry the boy home. He had such unselfish love and devotion for his son. And I must not forget your mother; every time Ivan was there with his son, your mother gave them a small bag of sandwiches and cookies to eat on the way home. I can't tell you how much they appreciated and looked forward to the bag full of food."

The good news about the offer of coal coupled with the remaining little bit of wood we already had led us to believe that we might survive until spring. This new development was a great relief to Grandfather. He had one less thing to worry about.

On another Saturday, after it had been snowing all day and night, the snow was still coming down in the morning. It came down heavy and fine, like a thick fog. I could tell by Mother's furrowed eyebrows that she was worried but she still was determined to go to the bazaar. At first, I was to go with her but because of the heavy snowstorm, Mother said, "This time I am going alone!"

Mother was worried about the bad weather and about the farmers who might not show up at the market. Their poor horses were weak from too much work and not enough food and they looked like old nags. One could count their ribs and hang a hat on their protruding hipbones. It was a sad sight. The horses plodded slowly under their heavy loads while the farmers whipped them to make them move faster.

We all suffered from lack of food, water and fuel but the animals, especially the horses, suffered the most at the hands of their masters. The farmers had no compassion for their beasts of burden who had served them so well and for so long.

After the snow set in and frost ruled Kiev, Grandfather observed one night, "Listen, can you hear it? I hear only silence. Where are the barking dogs and prowling cats? I suspect by now they have been killed and eaten by desperate people. One thing is certain, neither man nor beast can escape the suffering of war."

In the happy old days, before the occupation, going to the bazaar was a great treat for old and young alike. Usually, I had enough coins to buy some candy or a fruit or a cookie. The smells, sights and sounds of the bazaar are unforgettable; people hustled and bustled, friends greeted and hugged, farmers were friendly, produce was beautiful and plentiful and the handsome horses were there to be admired and patted. But after the occupation, people of all ages withdrew into themselves and became more like zombies, devoid of life. They came to the bazaar because of great necessity and they hurried home because of great fear for their lives.

That Saturday morning of the snowstorm, we waited anxiously for Mother. It was early afternoon before she appeared with a half-sack of coal and a huge head of cabbage. We were so glad to see her home safe that we forgot all about the bag. After many hugs and kisses, we remembered about the sack. When it was opened, we saw several lumps of black shining coal the size of a man's fist. There was joy and laughing and crying and hugging. We felt great relief because we believed that, thanks to Ivan we had found a source of fuel we could rely on for quite a while.

The next time Mother and I set out to go to the bazaar, we were smug in the knowledge that we would be bringing back a half-sack of coal. Before we got very far into the bazaar grounds, we saw a large circle of people screaming and gesticulating with hysteria. We heard words of accusation, derision and cursing. Still others were yelling to leave 'him' alone. But what was it all about?

We became a part of that big surging circle and, before we knew it, we had been pushed into the middle of the crowd. For me, it was like coming from darkness into the light; all those big people with their heavy coats had been pressing me so tightly I could hardly breathe, let alone see the sun. Now, the first thing I saw was a big brazen woman screeching, "Cut me a chunk, cut me a chunk!"

Then I heard Mother gasp for air. As if in slow motion, I looked where she was looking and I saw a dead horse hanging from a lamppost. Part of its body was skinned and carved while other parts were still covered with its own hide, stained with blood and dirt. Many women including Mother were covering their mouths with their hands and crying.

Once the pushing frenzy stopped, the buying frenzy started. Just like the brazen woman, most of the people were demanding a piece of the horse flesh. The farmer was trying to quiet the crowd down by assuring them that the horse meat was healthy for people to eat and was much cleaner than chicken meat. He said, "A chicken will eat almost anything, from rotten flesh to worms to its own droppings, but horses only eat clean grass, hay and grain."

Someone in the crowd yelled jeeringly, "By the looks of this poor nag, he has not eaten hay or grain for weeks."

Through their tears, everyone laughed hysterically. Normally, sadness and laughter are on the opposite ends of the emotional spectrum but in this case, laughter expressed deeply-felt pain. That morning, we all witnessed the unraveling of our civilized society as we knew it.

After all was said and done, Mother and I walked away with a piece of horse meat. I did not say a word but I wondered how I would be able to eat that poor horse? If I closed my eyes, I could still see him hanging above my head. Quickly, we picked up the meat and the coal and fled for home where we would feel safer.

When we got home, Mother handed the bundle of meat to Grandmother and whispered a few words in her ear. For weeks, I wondered every time we ate soup, "Am a eating that poor horse?"

But I did not want to know because I was hungry. Every time the soup spoon touched my lips, I could see the bony carcass hanging from the lamppost.

The prospect of a regular weekly supply of coal was a great boost to our morale. It was amazing how three lumps of coal could keep two rooms warm long enough for us to shed our gloves, caps, scarves and an extra layer or two of sweaters. We were able to sit at our kitchen table again like human beings and enjoy the simple pleasures of writing, reading and using our ungloved hands instead of staying in bed under the covers just to keep warm. Our spirits remained high and Grandfather seemed to feel better. With our immediate survival problems temporarily solved, Grandmother proclaimed, "We are blessed!"

The next Saturday after the dead horse episode, I refused to go to the bazaar with Mother. The sight of the dead animal had affected me deeply. When I was younger, I had flinched at the sight of blood or a squished bug. Now I faced the stark realities of life and death almost every day. I started to have nightmares about the suffering horse. With mixed feelings that morning, I stood at our window watching my mother disappear into a swirling snowstorm with my little sled trailing behind her.

By late morning, Mother was back with the coal, a head of cabbage and nothing else. No matter how scarce things were at the market, cabbage was always plentiful and cheap.

Mother looked pale and upset. When Grandmother asked her, "What happened?" She became even more agitated. She wanted to tell my grandparents something but she did not want me to hear it. This was almost impossible since we were cooped up in such tight quarters. They all knew I could hear everything. I was nicknamed 'long-ears' because I had such a keen sense of hearing.

My grandparents started to question Mother gently, "What did you see? What happened? Were you in danger?"

Finally, but reluctantly, the story came out. With tears, Mother said, "When I arrived at the bazaar where we saw the dead horse last week, I saw a group of people standing in a circle. But this time, they were silent and motionless. They all were looking up at the same lamppost where the dead horse was hanging last week."

Mother wiped her eyes and blew her nose and then went on, "I looked up and where the horse had hung, the farmer who just a week ago was selling the horse meat was now hanging.

"I could hardly take it all in," said Mother. "The farmer's eyes were popped out of his head and his tongue was long and blue. That was a pitiful sight, not because he was dead but because his body had been robbed of coat, shoes and socks. His feet were frozen stiff and blue, the same color as his tongue."

"Everywhere on the bazaar grounds there were

small groups of people grumbling and denouncing the Nazis," continued Mother. "Last week, they were angry with the farmer for mistreating his poor horse. This week, they were livid with anger at the Nazi soldiers for causing us such unbearable anguish. But most of their anger was directed at the anonymous citizens who had stripped the dead farmer's body of his clothes. The people were saying, 'They disregarded all respect for the dead. God will punish them!'"

There was a long moment of silence in our room. We were looking to Grandfather for answers. Finally, he spoke, "A person's need for self preservation is stronger than any moral code. After all, who needed warm clothing more? Was it the dead farmer who no longer felt any pain or the living men who were feeling cold and pain?"

The answer was obvious. Each of us was lost in our own thoughts. I was impressed with Grandfather's wisdom. I have never forgotten this new-to-me concept.

It seemed that there was more bad news every day and seldom was there any good news. We had become adjusted to living without electricity. After the German occupation, Kiev was in total darkness for weeks. Now, little by little the power had started to come back on. First, it came on in the heart of

Kiev where the Nazis' headquarters were clustered.

Next, the power service began to spread to the nearby city blocks. It had become clear to the Nazis that dark streets hid partisans and hoodlums. It was also easier for the Nazis to capture innocent citizens in the well-lit streets. So, one by one, the suburbs started to glow.

We knew the power would soon come to our neighborhood. One evening Grandfather said, "I can see you are excited about the power that will soon come to our neighborhood. But I see it as both good and bad. I think it would be better for us not to use the power at night just yet. As everything else, bright lights would draw attention to our windows and eventually to us."

Again, everyone was silent. We had been so hopeful. To us, the coming of power signaled a return to normalcy. But deep in our hearts, we knew Grandfather was right. Besides, we knew we would receive only enough power to light our rooms; we had no electric heaters, no cooking plates, no electric irons and our radio was still useless to us because the Nazis did not want us to know what was going on outside our world. So we all decided to go with Grandfather's suggestion and live as we had done before.

84   I Remember . . .

7. Grandfather's Last Days

By mid-December Grandfather was sleeping more during the days. In the afternoons, when Mother and Grandmother were busy in the kitchen, I watched over my dear grandfather. I would slowly tiptoe to his bedside and whisper, "Grandfather, are you asleep?"

He would smile and shake his head, "No, I am only resting my eyes." Then he would pat his bed with his hand; that was a signal for me to climb aboard. First, I would kiss him on his forehead and snuggle up to him as close as I could. Because I could not be still for long, I smoothed his eyebrows with my fingertips and slowly moved them over the ridge of his famous nose that curved to the right side of his face. Then my finger moved slowly and gently over his lips, barely touching them until that tickled him. He would blow air out through his closed lips, making a noise like a horse. Then we would laugh.

Whenever Grandfather and I did anything more

than once it usually became a ritual for us. So it was with the story telling. When I was smaller, Grandfather told me many stories. Now it was my turn to tell stories to him, the same tales he had told me so many years ago. We both loved our time together. Often, when I was telling my story, I saw Grandmother and Mother slip into the room quietly to listen and cry. At times like that, I wondered why they were crying. I was too young to realize that Grandfather was slowly slipping away from us.

Through the years, Grandfather told me many fairy tales, "Hansel and Gretel," "Little Red Riding Hood," "Sleeping Beauty" and many others. He told me stories about Ukraine, of farmers and villagers and about their hardships.

Grandmother, on the other hand, talked to me about different historic events and about people who made a big difference in our world. She often talked about famous women like Marie Antoinette and about young Spanish girls who had to suffer by wearing starched collars to stretch their necks so that their necks would be long and beautiful.

But the story I wanted to tell Grandfather the most was the same one I loved to hear when I was much younger and he told it to me:

КУРОЧКА РЯБА

ИЗДАТЕЛЬСТВО «МАЛЫШ» · МОСКВА · 1983

Nazi Invasion   87

The Speckled Hen

Once, there lived a Grandfather and Grandmother.
And they owned a speckled hen.
One day the hen laid them an egg.
It was not an ordinary egg but a golden egg.
Grandfather tried and tried to crack the egg but he could not.
Grandmother tried and tried to crack the egg but she could not.
A mouse ran past the egg on the table and switched her tail,
The egg rolled off the table onto the floor and broke.
Grandfather and Grandmother cried and cried,
But the speckled hen cackled.
Don't cry, Grandfather,
Don't cry, Grandmother,
I will lay you a different egg.
Not a golden egg,
But an ordinary egg you can eat.
Then Grandfather and Grandmother were happy.
They said, "Now we can have an egg for supper."

Preparing for Christmas

By the middle of December, 1941, despite bad news and shortages, Grandmother started to talk wistfully about getting ready for Christmas. She wished we could have a holiday like those we had had in days gone by. Grandmother wished for a tree with little candles clipped onto the branches, cookies and candies hanging from the tree limbs and our antique Nativity scene placed under the tree with a little bit of straw to make it look like a real stable scene where Jesus was born. She also wanted us to have a traditional Christmas Eve dinner with candles and wine. Mother tried to reason with Grandmother but she would not be swayed. Grandmother's tears broke our hearts and we decided to go along with her plan as best we could.

Grandfather was getting worse with each day and Grandmother was really worried. We needed help. We did not know what to do or where to turn. We were unable to make contact with Grandfather's doctor friend. We hoped he was well and safe wherever he was. Most of our friends had disappeared; we had no idea where they were. There was no hospital service, the pharmacies were closed and medicine was unavailable. We felt helpless! Mother and I learned later that Grandmother was suspecting this Christmas Season was going be Grandfather's last one. She wanted it to be special for all of us so we would have happy memories along with the heartbreaks that were yet to come. Grandmother was a great believer in the healing powers of chicken soup; that was a legacy passed down to our family by our Jewish friends. Grandmother insisted that Grandfather would get better if he could eat some chicken soup. With joy, she enumerated all the ingredients we already had, onions, carrots, and home-made egg noodles that we had made in the fall. The only thing we were lacking was a chicken. Grandmother and Mother agreed that chicken soup was our last resort to help Grandfather.

Once again, Mother was on a mission to trade some items for a chicken for Grandfather. I was all excited to go with Mother. At the last moment, Grandmother remembered that she had promised the night before, my help to our little neighbor, Rosa.

"She cannot see well and you know she lives alone. She needs help to sort her thread and buttons," said Grandmother.

I was torn between the prospect of buying a live chicken (in Europe, chickens are sold live) or playing with a box of beautiful old buttons. In the end, it was decided I would stay while Mother went on. The change of scene was good for me and for Rosa. I sorted the buttons to my heart's content and learned how to unravel an old white wool sweater and roll the yarn into fist-size balls.

By the time I returned home for lunch, Mother had already returned from the bazaar. Success was written all over her face. She had found a nice plump chicken with the help of Ivan; he was friends with all the farmers and knew what each of them had to sell. In addition to a half-sack of coal and four boiled "potatoes with pants on" (a Ukrainian expression for boiled potatoes with skins on) for our lunch, mother bought a nice plump chicken. Grandmother and Mother were all smiles but I was disappointed that the chicken was already dead.

Mother said, "I am so glad I do not have to kill the chicken." Sadly, I said, "I just wanted to pet the hen like I used to do when I was little." Then, the dam broke and my tears poured out like a flood. I sobbed inconsolably but I did not know why. My emotions were raw and I was overwhelmed. Mother sat down beside me on the bed to comfort me. Before long, she too was crying.

Meanwhile, Grandmother was finished with scalding and plucking the chicken. Water was boiling in a big pot. The hen was ready to be cut up, the onions and carrots were already peeled and cut up, and the noodles were ready. All the ingredients were waiting to be placed into the boiling pot of water.

Grandmother was not a stingy person; if someone was in need, she would give the shirt off her back. She was, however, extremely frugal. Nothing went to waste in her home. Therefore, nothing of the chicken went to waste except for the entrails, feathers and claws.

The aroma of that magical elixir was intoxicating; it made us hungry. I was convinced beyond any doubt that chicken soup would heal my grandfather but to be sure, I prayed, "Please God, make Grandfather well again!"

When the soup was ready, Grandmother took a partially cooled bowl of chicken soup to Grandfather. It looked wonderful and it smelled even better; we could see small pieces of chicken floating in the soup. It was so tempting that Grandfather ate his whole bowl of soup with zest. He said that was enough and did not want more.

We were happy with the results of our labor. We decided it would take more than one cup to make any improvement in Grandfather's health. We all had some of the soup, mostly the vegetables, noodles and only a few bites of chicken. The rest of the broth and chicken was stored in the unheated room to keep it from spoiling. Each day, after that, Grandfather had warm soup with noodles, vegetables and bits of chicken for his meal.

Just before Christmas, every time Mother and I returned from the bazaar, Grandmother was busy covering up and hiding things. Again, I could smell the wonderful aroma of days gone by; cakes, cookies and cooked meat. But Grandmother and Mother denied any knowledge of anything. They said in unison, "You are hungry for things we used to cook. It's your imagination that is hard at work."

Grandmother said, "You know we don't have anything like that in the house." Oh, they were good! They denied any knowledge of Christmas baking and I believed them.

Close to Christmas, our neighbor, Rosa, came over more often. She helped us in every way she could. Grandmother said, "She is lonesome for her family. Her children live in other parts of Ukraine and her husband was dead long before the war broke out."

Living alone in the time of occupation made Rosa vulnerable. She was isolated and lonely and also, in a way, she was trying to repay us for the help we had given her niece. Everything she did for us was an expression of her love and her gratitude to us.

One day, Grandmother said, "We can trust our little Rosa more than anyone else." This was a surprising statement coming from my grandmother, who didn't trust anyone except her family these days. During Soviet rule, people were encouraged to inform on each other. For that, they were rewarded with extra pay or free food coupons. No wonder people were suspicious of each other and did not trust anyone

Then Grandfather remarked, "Just think, how lucky we are to have each other in this time of great need. But our little Rosa has no one. She is alone. We need to remember that and try to help her in any way we can."

Grandfather was a compassionate and a perceptive man who often shone the bright light of wisdom on many issues in our life. His wisdom and clear thinking have helped me to remember and to understand what happened to us during those difficult last days in Kiev and the events that followed.

Christmas Day Arrives

I remember how just before Christmas, I was spending more and more time with our neighbor, Rosa. For one reason or another, I would be there. I was becoming better acquainted with Rosa and I was helping her do things that she no longer could see to do by herself.

Rosa and I had devised a plan for how I could go

to her place and return home comparative safely. On Christmas Eve afternoon, Grandmother asked me to go over and invite Rosa to have dinner with us. I thought, I'll go over, ask her to join us for dinner, and come right back. But when I got to her house, Rosa needed me to help her with several chores that took time.

Finally, she said, "If you wait for me, we will go to your house together." Then out of the blue, she wanted me to look at her photo album. I must admit, it was fun looking at pictures of her family. Her husband, whom I never knew, was tall and handsome. I saw photos her three handsome sons, their pretty wives and their small children. By the time we were finished, it was dusk.

"My goodness," said Rosa, "look, it is almost dark. Let us get some of these things into a bag and get going."

Quietly and quickly, we followed the route that had been outlined by my Grandfather. As soon as we came out of Rosa's back door, we took a deep breath, walked quickly past two houses and ducked into our back door where we let out a sigh of relief.

When we stepped into our kitchen, Grandfather was sitting at our big old kitchen table. He looked handsome and smiling, happy to see us safe at home again. Then I saw a big Christmas wreath, made of heavy evergreen boughs in the middle of the table. It was decorated with candles, shiny Christmas balls, cookies and candies. On each side of the wreath stood the figures from our antique Nativity set as if they were admiring the wreath. All around the wreath there were small packages prettily wrapped with bright satin ribbons. Everything looked festive and inviting. In a flash, I realized that the wreath had replaced our traditional Christmas tree but it was beautiful and we all were happy!

In our two rooms, the smell of good food reminded me that it had been a long time since lunch. To me, everything smelled and looked delightful but Mother and Grandmother reminded us how much better things used to be. All four adults had a glass of wine and even I had a tiny sip from Grandfather's glass. We had good tasting Borscht and pirozhki stuffed with meat and rice. After the Christmas dinner was over, Mother told me that the meat in our soup and in our pirozhki was horse meat. I closed my eyes and thanked the poor horse for his gift to our Christmas dinner and hoped he did not mind.

Each one of us got an apple, a piece of hard candy and some homemade sugar cookies. It did not take me long to recognize these sugar cookies. The previous September, before the occupation, Grandmother had baked them and I had helped to decorate them with green and red coarse sugar. Our Christmas dinner of 1941 was a modest meal but to us it was a wonderful feast and the memory of it has stayed with me all my life.

Before we started to eat, Grandfather said, "Let us thank our God for the way He has cared for us." We all bowed our heads. When the prayer was over, I saw Grandmother and Mother were wiping away their tears. Something else was strange about the prayer to me. I had not known that God was 'ours.' Looking back on those days, I realize now how biblically illiterate most of us were. To this day, whenever I see the words 'Our Father,' I am reminded of my first prayer in my grandparents' home.

The meal tasted every bit as good as it smelled. While the rest of us enjoyed the Borscht, without the dollop of sour cream, Grandfather had the last of his chicken soup. He never complained in front of Grandmother for fear he might hurt her feelings but when she was in the kitchen, Grandfather said, "I wish I could have some of your Borscht."

And he did! We were more than glad to share our Borscht with Grandfather.

After dinner we all sat back and relaxed. Grandmother gathered the gifts from the table and placed them into the basket. Then she handed the basket to Grandfather. With a big smile, he handed gifts out to each of us.

Mother received a small package. In it was a pair of pearl earrings. They were Grandmother's, a wedding present from her parents.

Mother was thrilled with the earrings but at the same time she was perplexed, "Where will I hide them. I want to save them for Lorissa's wedding." That Christmas Eve was the first and last time I saw those beautiful earrings. I am thankful that I had a chance to hold them even if for only a few minutes.

Next, Grandfather gave Grandmother a thick envelope and told her not to read it then. On the face of the envelope was written in big letters: "I love you now more than I loved you before. You have been the joy of my life. Thank you." Mother and I never learned what was in the envelope. We often talked about it in later years and speculated about what it was.

Next, Grandfather gave me a soft-feeling package. It was from Rosa. When I opened it, before I knew what it was, I recognized the wool from the white sweater that I had helped to unravel. Rosa had made me a white stocking cap trimmed in red yarn with a red tassel and a pair of mittens to match the stocking cap.

Grandfather gave Rosa a bag full of wool yarn

in many bright colors. She was surprised and absolutely thrilled. "Now I have something to keep me busy. Who knows, some day you may see this yarn made up into something you will wear," she exclaimed with a smile and tears of gratitude.

Mother gave Grandfather a special bottle of Ukrainian wine. It was to be saved until the day we were free again. Grandfather said to Grandmother, "Here, my dear, keep this bottle in a safe place where some day we will find it."

Grandfather asked to be put to bed, he was tired. He said, "Do not go yet, let us reminisce for a while about the days gone by."

Grandfather took the floor and we listened with pleasure as we were transported to another time and other places. We stayed up in the dark until late that night. When the party broke up Mother walked Rosa to her home. We waited anxiously until she was safely home again. Grandfather surprised us by his bitter remark, "We sneak around like thieves in the dark in our own land. Damn these Nazis!"

New Year's Eve and Day came and went uneventfully. But late that night, way past midnight, we heard several sets of Nazi boots pounding our sidewalk. Our hearts stood still. We were gripped with fear. The boots kept going back and forth, as if they were searching for someone. We laid still in our beds, afraid even to whisper to each other. The pounding became fainter and soon we heard several shots ring out in the distance. We felt relief wash over us but we knew that someone else paid a price for that night's peace.

Grandfather's 67th Birthday

Grandfather was born on January 1, 1875. Grandmother did not want to overlook his 67th birthday, especially since he had been feeling somewhat better. I was thrilled knowing that this time I would not be left out of the big surprise. The plan was simple but workable. We asked Rosa if she could bake a birthday cake for Grandfather if we provided all the ingredients.

Of course, her answer was, "Yes, I will be glad to."

Mother was able to find another chicken at the bazaar with the help of our wonderful Ivan. Ivan was always there for us in our times of need and we tried not to take advantage of him. To think Ivan's willingness to help us was all a result of my grandfather's kindness and compassion. Grandfather loved his compatriots and helped them every time he could.

On January 1, 1942, we celebrated Grandfather's

birthday. The lunch was simple but good. All of us, including Rosa, sat around the kitchen table enjoying chicken soup with sawdust bread. Grandfather ate his soup with gusto because we, too, were enjoying our own bowls of the same soup. Then he said with a twinkle in his eye, "No real Ukrainian man would be caught dead eating chicken soup; give him Borscht!" And then he winked at us. His joke was unexpected; we broke out in laughter to hide our tears.

Grandfather was really surprised and touched when Rosa brought in the birthday cake with a lit candle in the middle. The birthday party was the best thing we could have done for Grandfather. For about four days, his spirits soared. He was his old self; he slept less, ate more and seemed full of life.

A Death in Our Family

Just a few days later, January 6, 1942, Grandfather's health began to decline again. Grandmother and Mother were up all day and all night. They tended to Grandfather and kept him as comfortable as they could. He was coughing and for the first time that winter, rather than being cold, Grandfather was hot. During the day, our home was quiet. Everyone was busy and worried but no one was saying a word to me about Grandfather's condition. They had nothing to say since they themselves did not know what was really wrong with him.

On January 8, 1942, mother took me over to Rosa's while Grandfather was struggling to catch his breath. I was so upset. With tears and screams, I threw a temper tantrum, "I want to be with my grandfather! I want a chance to say good-bye to my grandfather!

But all Mother said was, "Give him a kiss for now and let's go."

I started to cry again and Mother said, "Stop it right now and do as you are told!"

With a softer tone, Mother said, "I promise you as soon as I can I will come to get you. Now be a good girl and do not cause any trouble for our little neighbor and help her as much as you can."

After six days, Mother came to get me. Dressed in black, she looked tired and downcast. When we returned home, I saw that Grandmother was dressed in black also. She was sitting on her bed softly crying. Everything in the room looked the same but somehow it appeared sad and different. A black crape cloth was draped over Grandfather's portrait but Grandfather was gone!

Grandmother and Mother sat me down on our bed and they sat down on either side of me. Lov-

ingly and tenderly, they told me that Grandfather
had died on January 14, 1942. I heard them but I
could not comprehend what they were saying. They
were heartbroken and so was I. I cried but still I did
not believe what I was told. Grandfather was my
invincible hero. In my mind and my heart, I knew
heroes did not die. Besides, hadn't I prayed to God
for Grandfather's healing? Looking back, now, I realize that I was in total shock and denial, refusing to
accept the reality of my dear grandfather's death.

When Grandfather died, there was no one to help
Mother and Grandmother with his body; there was
no one to pronounce him dead. They had to do it
all by themselves. So, according to the Ukrainian
tradition, they bathed Grandfather's body, dressed
him and carried him from his bed across the room
to place him on the dining room table. There were
no flowers in the whole city of Kiev during the war.
Outside our house, Mother gathered some pine
boughs and pine cones for decoration—that was it.

After everything was finished, Mother and
Grandmother, dressed in black, held a three-day and
three-night vigil for the man they loved so dearly.
There was no one to come to the wake the way they
would have in the days gone by. When friends and
relatives came to help, they brought food, flowers
and stayed for many hours to honor the dead and

commiserate with the living. I begged Mother to tell me what happened after Grandfather died. She was reluctant but finally she agreed.

Slowly and with a heavy heart, Mother said, "As Father lay dying, he could hardly breathe but he was more concerned about us than himself. He said, 'Do not worry about me. I am not afraid of dying. Remember all that I taught you. Be careful, be safe and live a happy life. Tell Lorissa, I love her and I will watch over her always.' Grandfather's thoughts and concerns, to the end, were for us."

"After my Father died, we were numb with sorrow and blind with tears," sobbed Mother. "At first, we were not certain whether he was dead or in a coma. But after many hours, we knew he was gone. I knew that preparing his body would be extremely difficult for the two of us. But we had no one else to help us or to guide us."

Mother continued, "When your Grandmother was a young woman, she helped her mother to prepare a body for a funeral. She knew what to do even though she was hesitant to try."

Mother paused and then said, "Eventually, Mother took the lead and I did whatever she told me to do. It was difficult but I do not regret even for one moment what I did for my father. I will never forget all we had to do for him that night."

I remember how I wanted to ask many more questions about Grandfather's last moments but Mother said, "Not now, I will tell you more some other time."

After the funeral our main concern was for my poor brave Grandmother. Soon other serious events demanded our attention and Mother never talked about Grandfather's last moments again.

The Funeral

I remember how on the day of Grandfather's funeral, Mother told me to dress warmly since the weather had turned bitter cold. We were in a hurry to get dressed, eat a small bowl of hot cereal and leave for the church. The three of us walked in silence with Grandmother in the middle, each of us with our own thoughts. After a while, I realized we were on the same street where Grandfather and I had walked so many times before. I remembered those glorious summer days as Grandfather and I walked joyfully hand-in-hand to the church. Suddenly, I was jerked back to reality! Grandmother slipped and almost fell on the icy sidewalk.

When we entered the church, we found several groups of people standing here and there. They were friends and former patients of my grandfather. Ivan was among them. (In the Greek Orthodox Churches, there are no pews in the sanctuary; able-bodied people are expected to stand during the service, but in back of the church there were a few benches for the very old.) A few of Grandfather's cronies were sitting on the benches. At the end of the service, his old friends came over to express their sympathy to us. Standing beside us was our neighbor, Rosa, who, by now, seemed like part of our family. All these people were there to say good-bye to their dear life-long friend. They all had disregarded the danger to themselves just to be at his funeral.

Immediately after we entered the Greek Orthodox Church, a priest came over to offer his condolences to us. Then he said, "People are dying by the hundreds every day. The funeral service must be short and the casket must be loaded on the next available hearse waiting in front of the church."

After the priest turned away, Mother broke down and cried. She said, "It is so unfair to the families. We will have no time to mourn for Father in the church he loved and attended all his life."

While all this was going on, I had located the casket in the center of the church. I was overjoyed to see Grandfather's profile in the casket. Dressed in his Sunday best, he was pale but so very handsome. I wanted to put my arms around him and give him a big kiss. But even though I was standing on my tiptoes, I could barely see him. Someone lifted me up—I think it was Mother—so I could touch his face. But the moment I made contact with my grandfather's face, I felt a jolt of shock course through my whole body, causing me to shiver. Grandfather's face was ice cold and hard like marble, not at all the way I remembered him, soft, warm and alive. The moment I touched him, my aching heart and my doubting mind knew without doubt that Grandfather was dead.

The funeral hearse turned out to be an old farm wagon pulled by two horses more dead than alive. It was impossible to find a decent coffin or hire a proper hearse during the days of the Nazi occupation.

I thought the horses at the bazaar were in bad shape but these poor beasts were so weak they could drop dead any moment. Besides being skinny, their legs were torn and bleeding. They stood shivering from pain and cold. Their suffering was unending. The pain of these horses was symbolic of what the Ukrainian people endured during World War II.

After the service, everyone went outside except for the men who carried Grandfather in his pine box casket, also, according to Ukrainian tradition. Outside, the weather was freezing and the sun reflecting off the snow was blinding to my tear-filled eyes. The driver mounted his bench and offered to let me ride with him.

Grandmother asked, "May we place this heavy bag beside my husband's coffin?" It was a dish of rice and raisins sprinkled with sugar. In normal times, after a body was buried, the traditional rice dish was left out on top of the grave. After the family left the cemetery, the needy came by and ate from the dish right there at the grave. This was a last act of kindness offered by the family on the behalf of the deceased.

The driver was a man of few words who grunted out some thing that sounded like, "Yes."

According to an old Ukrainian tradition, the family and friends usually followed the hearse on foot. Grandmother and Mother were to walk at the head of the procession. It was fortunate that the cemetery where our family plot was located was not too far from the church. Mother was concerned about Grandmother's health; she looked small, weak and worn out but there was no other way to get her to the cemetery. In pre-war days, there were buggies to rent for older and ailing people but those services were long gone.

As soon as the casket was loaded, the hearse started to move. I wished I was walking with Mother and Grandmother since it was freezing cold on top of the driver's bench. As time went on, I developed an urgent need to urinate but I felt trapped. No wonder! It had been five or six hours since we left our home that morning and in those days there were no conveniently located bathrooms along the route.

About half an hour into the procession, we approached an old railroad overpass where the hearse had to pass underneath. When we got closer to the overpass, the horses became visibly agitated. They refused to go any farther. In front of them was a partially frozen deep pothole containing icy water and jagged chunks of ice. It became clear to me and to everyone else who cared how these pitiful horses' legs had been cut. They had been forced to go over the same pothole back and forth many times a day for days on end.

At this point, everything stopped. The driver started to yell and curse the horses but they refused to move. In desperation, the driver started to whip the trembling animals mercilessly. Still they would not budge.

Out of nowhere, two Nazi soldiers came to the aid of the two suffering horses. When the people in the funeral procession saw the Nazi soldiers running toward them, they froze in place. Everyone expected to be shot on the spot. The soldiers were yelling at the driver, "*Du schwein-hund! Du schwein-hund!*" (You swine dog! You swine dog!) and many other German words of profanity.

One of the soldiers pulled the driver down off his wagon by the collar of his heavy coat, slugging the man with his fist about the face and head. One soldier took the whip from the driver's hand and snapped it in two. Then, he took time to pat and comfort the poor horses. The Nazi soldiers made the driver help them guide the terrified horses around the scary pothole. We all watched this with awe and fear. None of us could believe our eyes. We had not known there was even an ounce of kindness in the hearts of these murdering Nazi soldiers. To my amazement, everyone in the procession applauded the soldiers.

This was the first and the only time that these people witnessed any kindness from the Nazi soldiers.

In the middle of all this stress and excitement, I wet my pants and didn't even know when it happened. My underwear, my long, heavy wool stockings and the insides of my shoes were wet. It did not take long for my clothes to become frozen stiff on me. Walking became painful. The insides of my legs were raw from rubbing. In those days, Ukrainian women and girls did not wear long pants even when the weather was freezing cold. They wore skirts and dresses.

The funeral procession continued on to the cemetery, which was about ten minutes from the railroad overpass. At the green wrought-iron gates of the cemetery, all the traffic stopped. There was a long line of hearses waiting to unload. A cemetery caretaker was briskly moving from hearse to hearse giving out information to the grieving friends and relatives.

He said, "The cemetery is overcrowded with caskets as you can see. The ground is frozen solid and cannot be dug right now. All our able-bodied men are fighting on the front line. For now, we are forced to stack numbered caskets. When the weather turns warm and we are able to dig the ground, we will bury these bodies then."

It took a long time, but finally Grandfather's pine box casket was unloaded, numbered and stacked. Grandmother asked the caretaker if she could leave a dish of rice with raisins close to Grandfather's casket. The caretaker took the dish carelessly and walked away swinging it back and forth as he went.

Grandmother became even more upset. Just to think that there was no resting place for Grandfather that night was more than Grandmother could take.

The fact that the caretaker was so careless about the traditional rice dish added to her distress.

Mother was upset also but she had no time for her own feelings. She was too busy comforting and taking care of Grandmother. While we were trying to reassure Grandmother, there was a turmoil going on all around us. Some people were crying, others were asking for help and still others were angry with everyone and everything but no one was listening to them, no one was able to help them. We all were in the same boat. We each had to do the best we could for ourselves because there was no one to care about us.

Our hearse driver, bruised and swollen around his face and eyes, came up to us and urged us gruffly to hurry. He said, "If you want a ride back to the church, you better get on the wagon right now. I have several more caskets to bring to the cemetery tonight."

We asked the driver if our neighbor, Rosa, could ride to the church with us. He was upset and his first reaction was, "No!" But after a moment's thought, he relented and let her ride with us. The four of us climbed onto the wagon. There we sat on some dry straw, huddling tightly together to keep each other warm.

The sun began to set in the west and the coldness

intensified. Grandmother was shivering unceasing-
ly. The ride to the church seemed to last forever.
When we got there, the driver yelled, "Get off the
wagon. There is a casket on the sidewalk ready to
be loaded."

We tried to hurry but we were stiff with cold and
weariness. Grandmother was unable to move. We
helped her to stand up close to the wagon but she
immediately collapsed onto the ground. Mother said
urgently, "We must hurry, it is getting dark."

Grandmother kept begging us to leave her on
the sidewalk and go home without her. We all were
upset and crying. Finally, Mother got us organized.
We got Grandmother on her feet with Mother on
her right side and Rosa on her left side. I was to
hang onto Mother's coat so she could feel me at all
times.

At first, Mother and Rosa practically carried
Grandmother. Little by little, as her stiff bones lim-
bered up, Grandmother was able to half walk and be
half carried and we were able to move faster. Every
time we stopped to rest, Grandmother again begged
to be left behind.

Finally, Mother said to her, "You stop that! We
will not leave you here. If we leave you, you will be
frozen stiff in five minutes. We must keep moving
as fast as we can."

It was pitch dark when we arrived at the front of our house. Mother invited Rosa to spend the night with us but she wanted to go home to her own bed. When we stepped inside our two rooms, we realized they were almost as cold as the outside. Quickly, Mother got Grandmother into bed, told me to take my wet things off, find something dry to wear and get in bed with Grandmother so we could keep each other warm.

Mother lit a candle and made a fire. She brought us each a cup of sweetened hot tea. It tasted good after such a long day. We had been without food and drink for over eight hours. When we finished the tea, Mother brought us some sawdust bread and warm leftover soup. Grandmother did not want soup, she just wanted to sleep, but I ate everything that was brought to me.

The funeral day had been extremely stressful for all of us but especially for Grandmother. She slept for the next three days and three nights, getting up only to go to the bathroom and drink some hot tea with sugar.

The day after the funeral, I slept in until late. When I woke up, the sun was shining but it was still extremely cold outside. Mother was already up and dressed. The fire was going, our two rooms were warm and the hot cereal smelled good. Things seemed back to normal for me, except that my grandfather was gone. Only his portrait, draped in black crape cloth, a sign of mourning, was visible. I accepted the fact that he was gone for good but my heart ached and my hot tears bathed my cheeks. It was difficult to let go, I missed Grandfather so much. Our home was not the same without his presence. All three of us missed him in our own way. Grandmother missed her love and lifelong companion, Mother missed a loving father and a loyal friend, and I missed the best Grandfather a girl could ever have.

8. Life Goes On

After Grandfather's funeral, our concern shifted from Grandfather to Grandmother. For months during his illness, all our attention had been focused on him to the point that we had not noticed how much Grandmother's health had declined. She was thin, listless and devoid of that vital spark that had always been part of her happy-go-lucky personality.

The next time Mother went to the bazaar, she brought home a chicken for Grandmother. While we were plucking the bird, she said to me, "I can't stand the thought of losing my mother also. We must do everything we can to get your grandmother back on her feet."

From that day on, all possible care was lavished on Grandmother. For days, she did not respond to our efforts but by the end of January she began to come around. She was eating better and she even showed some interest in cooking and doing some light housework.

Since the funeral, our neighbor, Rosa, had been coming over more often to help us with Grandmother. She gave us invaluable advice on how to care for her. She volunteered to walk to the bazaar with Mother while I stayed home with Grandmother. On alternate weeks, Rosa stayed home with Grandmother while I had a chance to be out of the house.

While at the bazaar, we learned that there would be some rationed food distributed to the people of Kiev. All we had to do was register at a certain office to get the food stamps. On the day we picked up our bread, we were to receive also some butter, some sugar, dry beans and a little bit of tea. That was a great boost for the Ukrainian people in general and for us in particular since we were running low on the food that we had stored during the summer before the occupation.

When Grandmother began to come around, the first thing she wanted to know was what had happened to her younger sister Ulyana. We were astounded at her capacity to love her family even after all that she had been through. We had lost touch with Aunt Ulyana after the occupation but now Grandmother wanted to find her. As the matriarch of the family, she felt it was her duty to know where everyone was or what had happened to them.

The next week, when Mother and Rosa went to the bazaar, Mother took a great risk to put Grandmother's mind at ease. She went to Aunt Ulyana's apartment house while Rosa waited for her at Ivan's vending stall. Mother found out that the whole apartment complex had been looted, trashed and destroyed. Aunt Ulyana's flat on the top floor was totally demolished. Everything was gone, including light fixtures, door knobs, windows and doors. The new people who now lived close by knew nothing about Aunt Ulyana; it was if she had vanished into thin air. The news was hard for Grandmother to take.

"We neglected my dear sister, Ulyana." Grandmother's voice was sad and hollow just like her eyes. This was another reality we all had to face and move on from.

One mystery remained. Where was Grandfather's body? Mother had no choice; she went to the cemetery to put this agonizing question to rest and give Grandmother some peace of mind. Mother knew a friend, who knew a friend, who knew the superintendent of the cemetery. This kind man was able to answer our question. He said, "We have hundreds upon hundreds of coffins inside the cemetery gates and no able-bodied men to dig the frozen ground for burials. The coffins are stacked higher than the rock-wall fence around the cemetery grounds."

"You can see the coffins from here," he told Mother. "We are so back-logged that we have totally lost track of who is in each casket. We have no more secretaries to keep the records for us."

When mother got home, there was no way she could sugar-coat the stark facts about the cemetery. Silently and with dignity, Grandmother accepted the painful truth. Her tears had dried up a long time ago. Grandmother knew she was not the only one who had to face the cruel reality of life and death during World War II.

A Visit to the Old Cemetery

In August of 1995, while I was a Peace Corps Volunteer in Hungary, I traveled to Kiev to get in touch with my Ukrainian roots and to visit the cemetery where my grandfather was to have been buried. At the cemetery, I was ushered into a large office where a young lady named Mila was waiting to help me. Mila was eager to meet an American who had been born in Kiev 61 years earlier. We had a pleasant chat before we got down to business.

I told Mila all about my grandfather. That he had died on January 14, 1942, and was to be buried in section #1 of the cemetery. I said, "I bought a bouquet of flowers to place on his grave. I also need to have my grandparents' home address. Things have changed so much I can't find where their house used to be. I would like to see their place for one last time before I go back home to America. I would also like to have his official death certificate if at all possible."

Mila looked up the address for me and then told me that the street where my grandparents' home had stood did not exist anymore. During the Communist building expansion in Kiev, the whole neighborhood was torn down and in its place now stand four huge apartment buildings. Mila launched a search for Grandmother's death certificate but she could not find it. She did find a record book with a handwritten notation in pencil about Grandfather's date of birth, date of death and his home address.

Mila went on to say, "From the first of March in 1942, no more records were kept and there was no more lumber to build caskets. The frozen bodies were brought to the cemetery and stacked one on top of the other. Your grandmother must have died before that period of time and is stacked somewhere in section #1 but we have no other records than what I just gave you."

Then Mila said, "This brings me to the bouquet you brought for your grandfather. Since the mountain of corpses is higher than the rock wall and there are no paths to walk on without stepping on bodies, no one is allowed to go into section #1. After the Nazis left, we were unable to bury this mountain of bodies before another winter was upon us. These bodies have been decomposing and fusing into one solid block of organic remains for over 53 years. It was decided by the people of Kiev to let these poor souls rest in peace where they are now."

I thanked Mila for her help and offered her twenty dollars American money, which at that time was a lot of money. Mila hugged me good-bye, but she refused to take the money. She said, "I wish I could have been more help to you. You have come such a long way."

We stood on the cemetery grounds and through tear-filled eyes we looked at each other. I gave Mila the flowers that were meant for my grandfather. I told her, "Good-bye and good luck to you." Then I left that sad place with a heavy heart.

A Reversal of Roles

By the middle of February, life took on a semblance of normalcy for us; Mother, Grandmother and I were almost back to our old selves. We were more energetic and busy. In the evenings, when we went to bed, Grandmother took on Grandfather's role. She talked about the past and often answered questions about life in general, questions that I mostly asked.

One night, Grandmother said, "Well, Lorissa, do you have any questions for me?"

All day long I had been thinking what I would ask. In a flash, I asked, "Grandmother, why do we drink our tea from a cup and a saucer? When I play with Maria, her parents serve tea in a tall cup without a saucer?"

They were laughing at me again but Mother quickly came to my rescue, "That kind of cup, without a saucer, is called a mug and it is just as good as our cup and saucer."

Then Grandmother explained more fully about the cup and saucer. She said in a serious voice, "When the Communists took over Ukraine they took most of our prized possessions. They took our family antiques, furniture, clothing, dishes, and silverware. We were lucky, we still had enough dishes and furniture left to keep house. I tried, to the best of my ability, to set our table the way my mother used to do before the revolution. I refused to drink tea in a mug like a common worker and I hope my children and grandchildren will try to drink tea in a cup with a saucer in memory of me and my parents and the life we used to live."

Questions about the hate for Jewish people had been mounting in my mind. These were questions I was afraid to ask, since people often would only whisper about this subject.

One night I asked Grandmother, "Why do Ukrainians and Germans hate Jewish people? Why do Ukrainians often say in a Jewish accent, '*Oy Vey*, give me a piece of bread and a ton of butter?' What does that mean? "

My grandmother and other people I knew used this same expression when they talked about Jewish people. Grandmother said, "It is true, Ukrainian people often resented Jewish people. We all lived in the same country and we all suffered the same oppression under the Communist government. Yet, Ukrainian people starved while Jewish families had butter to eat during the same hard times. Butter represents the ultimate luxury in good and bad times. That is why Ukrainians cynically mimicked Jewish people by using the, '*Oy Vey*,' phrase so often. It has to do with the unfairness of life."

Grandmother went on to say, "My heart ached for our Jewish friends and neighbors when we saw them being driven like cattle down our street to the Babi Yar. We feared for the Jewish people and for what was in store for us. To this day, most of us regret the resentment that was festering in our hearts toward our Jewish friends. As a rule, Jewish people made good neighbors and good friends. They were honest and extremely hard working but they had a knack for choosing a good place of work that was the most helpful to them. Just look at our Jewish neighbors; one worked in the grocery store, one worked in the milk and butter store, one worked in the bread store and one worked in the pharmacy. This way, they were able to help each other with all the needs of life. None of us accused them of cheating or stealing. But, they knew how to make, spend and invest money wisely. Most Europeans suspected that Jewish people were wise. After all, they were the chosen people of God, as it is written in the Old Testament. This was what the Ukrainian people and the European people resented and feared the most."

On another night during our family discourse time, I asked Grandmother an important question. "I remember the first time you told me that I was chosen by God to be His own. How did you know God wanted me to be His own? How did He tell you? I have never forgotten that day in the kitchen, even though I did not understand it all. I always wanted you to tell me more."

Grandmother took a deep breath and said, "I have

always been of the conviction that God wanted you to become an Orthodox nun and to live in a monastery near Kiev to do His will."

As far as I was concerned, that sounded good to me. Nuns studied religion in preparation to do God's work and they served His church. The idea of wearing the elegant flowing black robe appealed to me. I was almost eight years old at the time and Grandmother insisted that God's will be done. When the subject finally came to a close that night, Mother took a deep breath of relief; soon we fell asleep.

When it was Mother's turn to ask questions, she wanted to know about our family roots. Who was married to whom, how many children they had and where did they live? What were their names?

Mother asked questions about her great-aunts and great-uncles. My mind became muddled with the unfamiliar names of old relatives and children I never knew. In all that confusion, I fell asleep.

I have always regretted I was too young to understand the importance of Mother's questions. I wish I could have stayed awake long enough to learn and remember the information about my distant relatives. That night I did learn one thing; most of my grandmother's family came from Odessa, the region near the Black Sea where the sun shines brightly and the sea water is not black but blue and warm and wonderful.

By the end of February in 1942, Grandmother became quite frisky. She was talking more and more about my upcoming birthday on March 15th. It was an exciting time for me. Every time Mother returned from the market with Rosa, she and Grandmother huddled in the kitchen, whispering with each other. On the days when it was my turn to go to the market with Mother, she kept her lips tight and would not tell me anything.

When I felt that unmistakable feeling of a cold or flu coming on, I did not dare tell Mother about my dreadful suspicions because that would keep me in bed. I did not want to miss the outing that was coming my way. For the next three days, I drank cups and cups of hot tea, hoping my cold would go away.

Mother said to me more than once, "What is the matter with you? You are drinking enough tea to float a boat."

But I just smiled at her sweetly and kept the secret to myself. At first, the tea seemed to work but the night before the bazaar, I knew my cold was upon me with vengeance. Still, I would not tell Mother that my chest hurt, my head hurt, my throat was dry and I ached all over. If only I had known what was in store for us on the upcoming day.

128   I Remember . . .

Part Two
Forced Exile

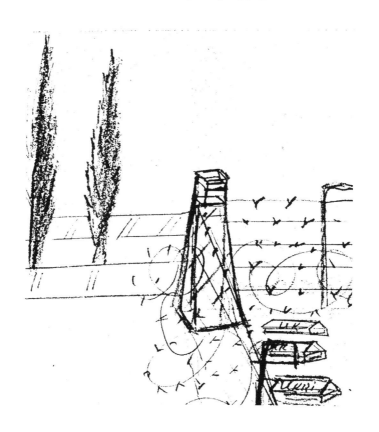

9. Captured

I remember the first Saturday in March of 1942, when Mother and I set out for the bazaar early in the morning. The sun was squinty-bright and the blue sky devoid of clouds. But the freezing cold air was mean to me, biting my nose and stinging my feverish and chapped lips. My throat hurt and it was getting more difficult to suppress my cough. Long before we got to the bazaar, Mother caught on to my secret. She was angry with me for not telling her the truth but it was too late to turn around and go back home.

She said to me, "I hope you are proud of yourself. Now you will have to be brave and endure physical discomfort while I'll have to hurry and get the shopping done."

Mother was really angry with me. She said, "You are walking too slowly. You cough too loudly and your nose runs without stopping. You knew you were sick, why did you forget your handkerchief?"

All in all, nothing went right. It was a miserable morning for me and Mother.

Ivan was not at his usual place but the other farmers had started to come in with their loaded wagons of produce and we knew he would not be far behind. Meanwhile, we walked around and looked for food items to buy. We had heard through the grapevine that some farmers were taking Russian rubles at a discount and at a great risk to their own lives. By now, most Ukrainians were aware that things were not going well for the Nazis on the war front. People of Kiev were hoping that the Communist government would return to power soon; that would make our lives much better and our rubles good. But we also knew that if the Nazi soldiers caught anyone bartering with Communist rubles, they would shoot them on the spot. Mother was hoping that someone would trade food for our rubles since we were running out of other things to trade.

We saw Ivan arriving at the bazaar in his red farm wagon. All at once, people were crowding in from all directions to barter for coal and wood. There was a lusty hum in the air, interrupted only by loud shouts of trading and laughter. On my little sled, we had already accumulated a half-sack of coal and some food items, including a large cabbage head.

I could tell that Mother was beginning to have

pity for me when she said, "As soon as we find three boiled potatoes for lunch, we will be on our way home."

It was too early to buy hot potatoes. Potatoes in boiling water were brought to the bazaar in large galvanized buckets in late morning. While we waited in line for our turn, all I could think of was my warm bed and my cozy home.

Out of nowhere, five huge Nazi trucks rolled into view. With screeching tires, the trucks braked to a sudden stop and formed a circle around the bazaar. Immediately, the soldiers, as if synchronized, jumped out of the trucks to infiltrate the shopping area. They descended on the bazaar like the black plague with death in their eyes. These hateful Nazi soldiers held their bayonet-mounted rifles ready to shoot or stab anyone they wished. Their vicious dogs were at their side eagerly awaiting a command to attack.

As soon as the Nazis were in control of the Plaza, they began to herd certain people closer to the trucks and they started to yell, *"Mach schnell! Mach schnell!"* (Hurry up! Hurry up!) The dogs were snarling and lunging at anyone who came within their biting range. As if they were in a hurry, the soldiers started to load the frightened people into the trucks.

It soon became obvious that they were looking

for strong young people, who were mostly women and older children, including Mother and me. A teenage girl was thrust into the truck while her elderly grandfather was pushed aside. The weak old man became panic-stricken at the thought of losing his granddaughter and ran to the truck in an attempt to rescue her. A big Nazi soldier used the butt of his rifle to strike the old man back with all his might. The old man staggered backwards and his body slammed into the packed snow and ice with great force. His head exploded like a watermelon; blood spurted out and made a red halo around his head on the snow. I could hardly look through my tear-filled eyes at the nice old man who was lying dead on the snow for no reason at all!

First Burst of Outrage

I had seen other atrocities committed by the Nazis before but this was more than I could take. Deep in my heart, such a hot hatred against the Nazis had been kindled that I could no longer keep silent.

All of a sudden, I stood up on the bench in the truck and screamed at the top of my feverish lungs, "I hate you, I hate you! Somebody, kill them! Kill them!" My heart was breaking for our people and my tears came down like a flood.

All at once, that day, I understood the true nature of our Nazi enemy. Until then, war had made no sense to me. Until then, I had stood on the outside feeling untouched by all the madness and cruelty that I saw the Nazis dishing out. I did not know the old man and his young granddaughter but this latest atrocity was too much for me. This man's death and his granddaughter's pain became too real and too personal for me. Their pain became my pain.

Mother pulled me down from the bench and covered my mouth with her hand but my hot tears kept falling. Everyone in the truck was alarmed. They thought I would be shot. The thing that saved me was the fact that the Nazis did not understand Ukrainian and they thought I was a harmless little girl. They were busy starting their trucks and pulling out from the outdoor bazaar.

Later on, Mother said, "After I pulled you down, you became limp and fainted."

I did not remember fainting but as I look back at the events of that day, I am amazed over and over again at how meek and mild we all were; we were like lambs being led to slaughter, meek and submissive! No wonder the people in the truck were surprised and alarmed at my outburst. So was I.

Most of the people in our truck were convinced we were being taken to Babi Yar and we knew what awaited us there. No one can imagine how terrified and helpless we felt. As our truck started to pull away, we saw Ivan holding my little red sled and yelling from the crowd, "Do not worry, I will help your grandmother."

Mother and I sat on the truck bench like two limp dolls drained of all our energy. All we could do was cry and cling to each other. We had no idea where we were going, what would happen to us and who would care for Grandmother. I was so sorry and I deeply regretted not telling Mother that I was ill. We might have stayed home that day and escaped being captured. That way, I could be the one to care for my grandmother. Our only hope was that our neighbor, Rosa, and Grandmother would somehow bond together to help each other to survive.

10. The Cattle Cars

As the truck traveled down the road, the people started to murmur, "This is not the way to Babi Yar! But where are they taking us?"

Someone shouted, "They are taking us to the industrial train tracks. I can see cattle cars waiting for us on the side tracks."

When our truck arrived, there were other Nazi trucks already unloading people captured from other parts of Kiev. As soon as our truck came to a stop, we were shoved with brute force out of the vehicle. A couple of Nazi soldiers were trying with all their might to slide open a rusty side door on the cattle car. I was pushed into the empty cattle car and the contrast between bright sunlight and the smelly, deep-black hole of the cattle car was blinding. All around me, I heard people softly sobbing and crying, "Oh, my God, oh, my God!" We felt trapped with no way out.

Standing in that dingy cattle car, I foresaw destruction for us all. I experienced a numbing fear of death and my heart was filled with unbearable sorrow for my mother, my grandmother and me. Our whole family was in peril, each of us in her own way.

As our eyes adjusted to the murky dusk, we saw that the cattle car walls were covered with dried-up streaks of runny manure and the floor was littered with large dried-up chunks of dung. And in the middle of all this was a large pile of what appeared to be clean straw. While we stood taking all this in, the sliding door was slammed shut with a bang. We found ourselves trapped in the cattle car, which was now even darker than before. High above our heads there were slit-like windows, four or six on each side of the car.

Mother told me, "Just before the train left the station in Kiev, Nazi soldiers had opened our sliding door and handed each of us a tin mug. That gave us some hope that food or water would be coming soon."

Mother tried to tell the soldiers, "My child is sick with fever. She needs water." They would not listen. Pushing her roughly aside, they said, *"Ich verstehe nicht.* (I don't understand.)"

Later that night, as the train slowly pulled out from the sidetracks onto the main line, some of the people got down on their knees and prayed to God for help and deliverance. Others were softly crying good-bye to Kiev and still others stood on the shoulders of their friends to take a last look at Kiev through the high window slits. All of us were hungry. We had had nothing to eat since early that morning. Moreover, we did not know when our next meal would come. We needed to use a bathroom but most of us were too modest. So, with legs crossed, we waited until the dark.

Much of what went on the first two or three days, I do not remember. I was burning up with fever and I slept for three days and three nights. The only thing I asked for was water but even water was unavailable.

Later, Mother told me about the first few days, how the captives divided the straw and how one of the women pulled up a loose floorboard in the corner of the cattle car for bathroom purposes.

Since I was very sick, the people decided that Mother and I should have a corner of the cattle car where there was extra straw. We sat and slept on the floor. There was nothing in the car but people, straw, a bad smell and the high window slits above us. When it was sunny outside, the light came through those window slits like laser beams. I sat on the floor and pretended that this sunlight beam was a stairway to heaven, a way for us all to escape. One day, I reached out to see if the stairway was real. I was heartbroken when I retracted my hand. A cold chill enfolded me and the reality of our situation became clear to me. We are doomed! I thought.

It took a while for the people in our cattle car to realize this, that we were all doomed. We had no washing facilities, no bathrooms, no heat, no blankets and no food. We had no change of clothing; what we had worn to the market was all we had. When it was sunny, our cattle car warmed up a little and then the lice came out. They moved to our foreheads and down to our eyes, trying to get some moisture. Most of the people had never had lice before. All of us were absolutely horrified but there was nothing we could do about the lice. The nights were still brutally cold and we all were desperate to keep warm. Though we were strangers, we huddled together at night, body to body, for warmth.

There were no Nazi soldiers riding with us in our cattle cars so the people felt free to speculate on what might be our fate. Most thought, if we were being taken to Germany, that we were traveling through Poland. Some thought we were being taken to a German concentration camp; others that we might be taken to work camps. Still others said that we might be on our way to Treblinka, one of

Poland's most inhumane camps.

Everyone was sad and downcast; no matter where we were going, our future was bleak with no hope for survival. But rather than dwelling on our impending demise, we tried to think of ways to escape. Night was the only possible time to go.

One woman said, "We could enlarge the hole in the floor then jump out of this cattle car and run."

This seemed like a good idea, until we thought about it. We would not know were we were and how far we had to go before we could find some one who could help us. That idea was put on hold.

A New Family Member

I remember Mother talking about the cold that first night in the cattle car. She often said, "I would not have survived without Lorissa's feverish body heat. Her fever was high and there was nothing I could do to help her. All night long, I just cuddled close to her to keep warm and prayed for Lorissa's health and safety."

Olga, the teenage granddaughter of the old man who had been killed trying to protect her, befriended Mother and me. Olga slept on one side of Mother and I slept on the other side. Most of the time, Olga stayed close to us. She felt lost and she missed her dear grandfather.

Olga told us her mother had died four years earlier and her father was somewhere on the Russian front fighting the Nazis. She lived with her grandparents just as I had the last few years. Olga was an orphan now and Mother was kind and sympathetic to this lost young girl who often cried quietly so no one could hear her during the night.

One day, Mother said, "Olga and Lorissa look just like sisters. They both are blonde and only three years apart in age."

Olga was about twelve and I was almost eight. I had forgotten about my approaching birthday during our terrible ordeal in the cattle car. And so, in these desperate times and awful conditions, Mother and I accepted Olga as family; nothing else around us was making any sense.

From day to day, we had no idea where we were. None of us had a watch to tell us what time of day it was. We were helplessly lost in every sense of the word. One day, sometime around noon, the train stopped and we heard a noisy commotion down the line. We heard the cattle car doors being slid open and then shut again after a short time, one after another. We had no idea what was going on. We heard angry voices of Nazi soldiers saying, "*Mach schnell! Mach schnell!*"

Soon our doors slid open and we were told to jump down. "*Mach schnell*," the same angry voice commanded. Later on, we learned that in most cars there were a few men along with women and children while in our car there were no men. The men were directed to one side of the cattle car and the women to the other side where they had to squat down and relieve themselves on the ground. In our car there were only middle-aged women, two teen-age girls and several grade school girls so the soldiers made us stay on the same side of the cattle car to relieve ourselves. We, who were raised to be extremely modest, felt deeply humiliated and painfully embarrassed to do our most private chore in full view of young Nazi soldiers who stood laughing and staring at us.

Again, the rage rose up in me against my enemy, but without any chance of resolution and without hope. I realized that my future was in the hands of these murderous Nazis who had robbed me of my country, my immediate family, my home, and now my dignity.

Then, with the same stern order of "*Mach schnell!*", we were herded back into our cattle car. Next, we heard the loud clatter of tin on tin which meant that soon we would eat. Once a day, we were fed a tin cup of thin vegetable soup and a piece of dry black bread or a hot boiled potato; sometimes we just had soup made out of potato peelings and other kitchen waste.

As the days went by, we saw that our train moved slower and slower. We traveled mostly by night and parked on side tracks during the day. Through cracks in the walls, we heard and saw luxurious looking foreign passenger trains full of Nazi soldiers speeding by, fast like a bullet. The passenger trains traveled in both directions.It did not take long for us to figure out that the railroad tracks had to stay open for troop transport during the day. During those days, we had nothing to do but huddle close to each other to keep warm, sleep and talk. One day, the talk turned to the subject of our abduction.

One woman said, "Did you notice at the market, while we were being rounded up and loaded into the Nazi trucks, the farmers were left alone. They acted as if they knew they were safe."

Another woman said, "That's because the Nazis need farmers to feed their army. The farmers who worked on big farms were told by the Nazis, 'If you provide what we need, you will live'."

The first woman said, "The Nazis took all that was the best from the farms. They killed our best cattle, they drank our good milk, they killed our chickens by the hundred and still they expected eggs. That is why we could not buy milk for our babies or eggs for our sick elderly at the market."

Someone challenged the women. "How do you know all this?"

The first woman replied, "That is easy; my brother and his wife lived and worked on a large collective farm established by the Communists. My brother was the one who told me."

Another woman said, "Do not forget that all of our grain is gone. Carload after carload of grain was loaded up and taken to Germany from the first day of occupation. That is why we ate sawdust bread instead of the black bread that we love. We live in the land that is called *the bread basket of Europe* but, little by little, we all are starving."

Someone else said, "Don't forget that armies travel on their stomachs. That is why food is so important whether it be to the Nazis' Army or to the Communists' Army."

That conversation was an eye opener to me. I had never given much thought before to where our food and grain came from or where it went. But I have never forgotten that lesson. Grandfather was right when he said, "Lorissa, you are like a sponge as far as learning is concerned."

As days went by, the weather turned noticeably warmer. The sun hid behind the clouds and instead of snowing, it began to rain like a torrent for several hours at a time. Then, after taking a little break, it rained again.

Fearful Virgins For Lecherous Soldiers

I remember how one morning we heard the sliding doors being quickly opened and shut down the line. We thought it was time for food but instead, several young Nazi soldiers climbed into our car and started to look around. Soon they spied one teenage girl and then they saw Olga. They pushed the girls into a corner of the cattle car and after a moment's thought they decided to take me also. The Nazi soldiers told us to *"Mach schnell"* and jump down from the train.

As we walked away from the train, we heard the mothers in our cattle car and in other cattle cars wailing and beating their fists against the doors. They called out our names in a pitiful and loving way.

The Nazi soldiers hurried us into a nearby railroad building. Once inside, we came face to face with eight well-dressed and well-fed Nazi officers. They greeted us politely with eager smiles and greedy eyes. One of the officers, who seemed to be in charge, said pointing at us, *"Sie bist schmutzig."* (You are dirty.)

The soldiers told us to undress. That struck terror in our hearts! But we did as we were told. As soon as we were undressed, they told us to line up. We were shaking from cold and fright. Some of the older girls noticed that there were other soldiers peeking at us through the holes in the wall; in a whisper, that news was passed on from girl to girl. Olga and I clung to each other for warmth and to cover up our nakedness. We seemed to be more shy and modest than the rest of the girls who looked older.

When the officers came out of their office, they had a greedy gleeful glint in their eyes. They stood rubbing their hands and smiling like hungry wolves. The sight of them made my heart stand still. I feared for my life as I never had before. The Nazis looked carefully at each older girl and then their attention turned to me. They laughed hysterically at the sight of me saying, "*Was ist das?*" (What is this?) They pointed out all my physical defects. Then they said that I was too small and my legs were too skinny and my knees were too bony. They laughed and poked at my flat chest and at my runny nose with their leather-covered riding quirts.

The close inspection by the Nazi officers terrified me. Their cruelty caused me to cough uncontrollably until I gagged. Green mucus ran from my nose and pus-filled tears ran from my eyes. I had nothing to wipe my face with so I used my naked arms and then I rubbed my arms against my body. It was awful! The sight of me made the officers sick. They pretended to gag and then they laughed. One of the officers commanded a soldier to take me back to the cattle car. The other girls were ordered to go into the next room where they were to take a shower.

While I was hurriedly dressing, I could hear the girls in the next room taking showers. I heard their sad cries and it was the most mournful sound I have ever heard. The soldier was angry with me and he yelled repeatedly for me to "*Mach schnell!*" Each time, his voice became louder and angrier then it had been the time before. I had no time to do anything but throw on my clothes and leave, even before I had laced my boots.

At that time I was too young to fully understand what was going on. A week earlier, I had witnessed the murder of Olga's grandfather and I expected the same fate to befall the girls and me in the railroad station. That is why I was so relieved to be back in the cattle car with my mother and the other people. I felt so grateful to be safe and sound, if only for the time being. I had no idea what was going to happen to the other older girls.

Ukrainian girls were raised by their strict, straight-laced mothers to be aware of the dangers of this world. These girls knew well that virginity was everything to a young Ukrainian girl. They were warned to be on guard against rape by strange and dangerous men. During the time of war in Ukraine, there were no more dangerous men than the Nazi soldiers.

I knew when I left the cattle car, by the way my mother was crying, that Olga and I were in great danger. I was lucky to escape unscathed, thanks to my illness, my small size and my sad physical condition. Many years later, when I was a teenager, it dawned on me what that incident was all about. I now understand more fully the danger we faced and how fortunate I was to escape. To this day, I mourn the loss of those innocent, young virginal lives. Those girls did no harm to anyone and yet, no doubt, they suffered a most degrading and painful death at the hands of sex-hungry Nazi monsters. As far as I know, all those eight girls, including Olga, were never seen or heard from again.

II. The Holding Camp

I remember how we continued to travel for two more nights after that last stop. Then, on the third night, the unexpected happened. Shortly after midnight, the train stopped and we heard the sliding doors banging open down the line. We heard the Nazi soldiers bellow the same old phrase, *"Mach schnell!"* We also heard their mean dogs barking as they strained against their leashes. This told us that we were being joined by other Nazi guards. Everyone in our cattle car was trying to peer through the cracks to see what was going on. Some of the people said they could see a faint light in a distance.

And then, it was our turn to *"Mach schnell!"* and jump down from our cattle car. We were scared and reluctant to leave the terrible cattle car where at least we had been safe from harm, all except for poor Olga.

We were ordered into a tight formation and told to march. I was surprised at how long the column was; some said there were more than 250 of us. It was raining and the dirt road was muddy and pot-holed. The night was pitch-dark and the only light we had came from the Nazis' darting flashlights. Every step was a gamble; would it be mud or ankle-deep ice water?

Walking was a struggle for all of us but we per-severed, wondering about our fate. As we walked, we whispered to each other, "Where are they taking us? Are we in Germany or in Poland?" But no one knew. We were weak from starvation and cold from the elements. On top of all that, some of us were sick, including me. We marched as fast as we could because we knew the alternative could be death. I do not know how long we walked but it seemed like forever.

Finally, in the distance, we saw lights getting brighter and closer as we trudged through the mud and water. We were stopped in front of a crudely-made, heavy-duty gate strung with barbed wire. We saw several high watchtowers and there was more barbed wire everywhere we looked. The blinding lights were shining down on us from the towers. In-side the fence, there were many long wooden bar-racks with small narrow windows.

As soon as we were inside the camp, a Nazi officer in charge started shouting out orders. The soldiers separated the new inmates into groups of fifty, causing real chaos as families were split up and herded into separate groups. The mothers were crying and children were screaming. One pregnant woman fainted, landing right in the middle of a large mud puddle. When the commander saw that there were very few children and hardly any men, he changed his mind and decided to let the families stay together. As far as I can remember, this officer was one of a very few kind Nazis I came in contact with during my long and unbelievable journey.

The Nazi soldiers led us into long buildings with bi-level shelves that served as beds on each side of the room. There were two long tables in the middle of the room but no chairs. I remember wondering how a table could be used without chairs. We were ordered to go to bed right away. There were no blankets but there was an ample supply of used straw to lie on. The next day, we were issued one blanket each. The building was cold but, still, it was much warmer than the cattle car. Even though we were wet from head to toe, there was nothing we could do about it but try to fall asleep.

While we were getting settled in, a Nazi soldier came in with a large box full of big chunks of bread. With the aid of his hands, he told us, "Everybody was to take two pieces of bread and go to sleep."

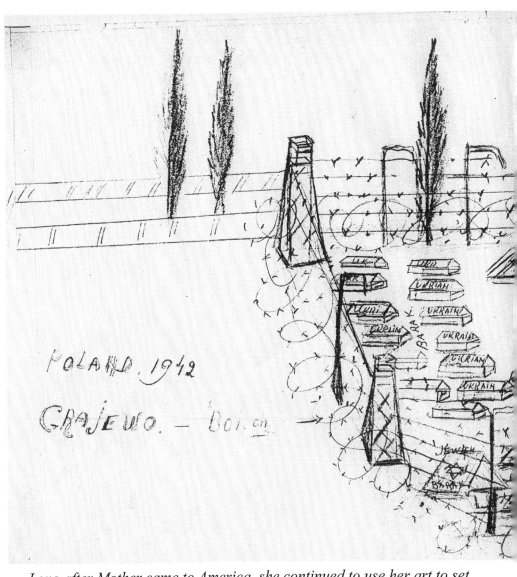

Long after Mother came to America, she continued to use her art to set
herself free; but the black memories of her past would not release her. This
sketch depicts the Nazi holding camp near Grajevo, Poland. To her dying day,
Mother believed the camp's shower room was meant to be a gas chamber.

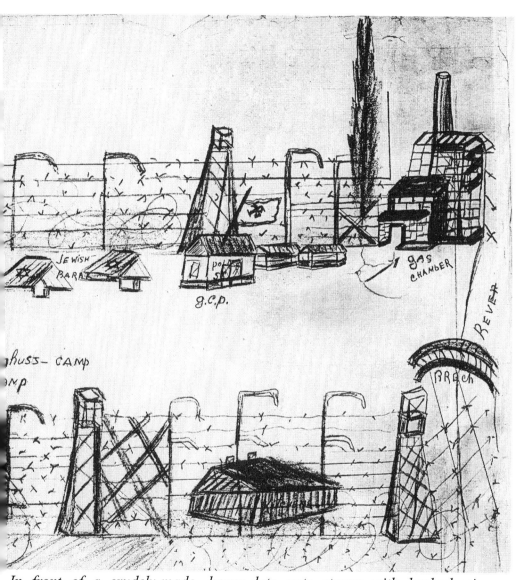

In front of a crudely-made, heavy-duty gate strung with barbed wire, we saw several high watchtowers and there was more barbed wire everywhere we looked. Inside the fence, there were many long wooden barracks with small narrow windows.

We were thrilled with our two large pieces of bread because we had not expected anything at all that night. Finally, the lights in the building were turned off as if by magic. We went to sleep eating our precious bread and snuggling with each other to keep warm.

In the morning, Mother and I awoke early and were looking around but we were afraid to speak. Next to mother was an elderly couple. They were kind and friendly to us. From the start, I liked them. Our attention turned to a commotion going on outside. From our little window we could see people walking in groups with Nazi soldiers watching them. They were coming and going from somewhere. Later we learned that they had been going to get their meals.

Shortly after that, a Nazi soldier came into our building accompanied by a young lady dressed in similar uniform. The soldier had a small box in his hands and from our second level bunk I could see there were yellow stars on pieces of dark cloth in the box. The young lady could speak Ukrainian and German. The Nazi was telling her what to say.

She asked, "Are there any Jewish people in your group. We have these yellow stars for you to wear. We want to be able to tell you apart from the rest of the people."

In one voice, the people replied, "We have no Jewish people among us!"

They showed us the location of restrooms and water faucets. We were told that we would eat in the morning and in the evening. We had to take our tin cups with us and go to the kitchen window. We would be escorted by a soldier each time. I think they let us sleep in a little that first morning; after that, we were up early. It was still raining and the grounds looked like a swamp. I dreaded to get my feet wet again, since my almost-dry boots were old and water would seep in quickly.

First chance Mother had, she pulled me aside and said, "I think the couple who slept next to us is Jewish. Don't say a word, but, as soon as we can, we need to get away from them."

We could not talk any more that morning even though I had many more questions to ask. I wanted to know how Mother could tell that they were Jewish. The unanswered questions left me confused and one more thing to be scared of. I knew what the Nazis did to the Jewish people in Kiev but that was too scary for me to contemplate.

After that short whispered conversation, there never was a good time for us to distance ourselves from the Jewish couple. We continued to sleep in the same place. I do not know how long we stayed at that camp; it must have been weeks.

People in our barracks were saying, "This is not a real concentration camp. It is a holding camp, a warehouse of human beings. From here, people are shipped, as needed, to German factories as workers or to one of the many concentration camps in Germany." It was as if we were standing before two doors; behind one door could be a concentration camp and behind the other door could be servitude in factories and who knew where else. Our lives hung constantly in a balance; cruel servitude or death.

Death By Lightning

In mid-spring, there were strong thunderstorms in that region—by now, we knew we were in Poland. One night, bolts of lightning were striking all around us. One lightning bolt entered a room through a window and killed a man sleeping on a table under the window. The camp was overcrowded and people were sleeping wherever they could find room. This terrible disaster happened in a barracks next to ours. At first, everyone was spooked. Some said, "Even nature and God are against us. What did we do to deserve this?"

After seeing so much suffering, I began to wonder if I was responsible for these occurrences. Had I done something to bring on this terrible catastrophe? I did not know much about God. What I heard about Him inclined me to believe that He was a God of vengeance and not a God of love as I learned later in America.

But it did not take long before the good people of the camp turned into wild animals. For the second time in my life, I witnessed human nature at its worst. Before the dead man's body was cold, the people started to rip off his clothes. They fought over his shoes and his belt, the most prized items. Only the strongest walked away with anything.

I stood watching them and I cried. I remembered what Grandfather had said to me when I was so upset about the body hanging from the lamppost in Kiev being robbed of its shoes and socks. "Don't judge them. The living have a greater need than the dead. What good are the shoes and socks to a dead man?"

The weeks turned into months and I lost track of time as we dragged ourselves through day after painful day.

The Gestapo Takes Mother Away

I remember how one day, totally unexpectedly, a Gestapo officer came and took Mother and the Jewish couple away. Nobody knew why or where they had been taken and I was left all alone. Almost overnight, I became invisible to everyone. I missed my mother and my concern about her well-being grew. My heart ached for both of us. The other people in the camp did not want to associate with me for fear of guilt by association. I could not understand what was happening to me or why. For the first time in my life, I was separated from everyone I knew and loved. I was alone with no one to love me or care for me.

12. Deliverance

In March of 1943, I turned nine without even re-membering my birthday. One morning, after we had been fed, I did not go back to the barracks. Lost in my thoughts and drowning in sadness, I went for a walk instead. I stopped in a sunny spot by the gate to warm up. Just at that time, a pickup was leaving the camp. It was driven by a man who wore a uni-form like the one worn by the Polish girl who had interpreted for the Nazi soldier when we had first arrived at the camp. The pickup driver reached out and pulled me into the cab before I even realized what was happening. He took me to his home where I met his pretty young wife.

After a hurried conversation between the two of them, they made me understand, by the use of their body signals, that her name was Maria and his name was Paul. Then they showed me their wedding rings to let me know they were married. In turn, I told them, with the aid of my hand signals, that my name was Lorissa. They said it was a pretty name. Then, they pointed at me and said that I was pretty. I did not understand most of what was being said but I understood that we were trying to get acquainted. To make me feel more comfortable, Paul and Maria fed me and let me sit in a comfortable chair by a stove to warm up. Before long, I fell asleep.

Two or three weeks later, I still could not speak or understand Polish well enough to ask any questions. But I was happy to be in this friendly home even though I did not understand what was going on. I was worried still about my mother but I could not help hoping my own good luck would last forever.

Those first few days, for the most part, were silent and uncomfortable. I was eager to observe, learn and please my new friends. I could see they were a kind and loving family.

I was afraid that if they did not like me, they might send me back to the camp where I had no one to care about me. The unkind people there had totally ignored me because they were more concerned about their own safety than about the welfare of a small girl. Mother was not there to miss me and make a fuss about my disappearance and those cold, heartless people did not care about where I was or what might have happened to me. I had just disappeared and hardly anyone had really noticed. Those who did were just relieved I was gone. The population of the camp was in a constant flux; some people were brought into the camp and other people were sent out. Who would miss one little girl?

Winter turned into spring and thanks to Grandfather's teaching, like a pro, I was able to tell the signs of spring. The trees and flowers were beginning to bud and bloom, the birds were singing and life was beautiful and new again.

I had been with Paul and Maria for over two months and all this time, I secretly worried about my mother and often cried into my pillow at night so Paul and Maria would not hear me. One day, I asked Paul if he knew anything about my mother. He just shook his head and looked at me with his sad brown eyes.

Then, a few days later, Paul told me, "It will be dangerous for me but I will try to find out where your mother is and if she is still alive. I cannot promise you much more than that."

I threw my arms around his neck and, with tears of gratitude, I thanked him for all he had done for me.

I do not know when I began to understand some of the words being said to me in Polish. At the same time, Maria and Paul quickly picked up on my ability to understand them. We all were thrilled. From then on, they watched for my reactions to what they said. Paul would say to Maria, "Lorissa is a pretty girl." At once, my face would turn red; it was a giveaway that I had picked up on his meaning. After that discovery, communication began to get better with each day. One day, without planning, I uttered a whole sentence in Polish. I was surprised and thought to myself, how did I do that?

As the weeks passed, my Polish-speaking ability improved rapidly. The news that I had leaned to speak Polish spread all through the village. The people of Grajevo (the name of the village) were proud of me. They thought I was a smart young lady. But I wondered how did I learn to speak Polish so quickly? Mother had told me over and over again that I was stupid and I believed her. All I could say to anyone who asked was, "I do not know how I do it but I am glad I am able to talk to you."

In June of 1943, I was about three months past my ninth birthday. I knew nothing about linguistics or about the Slavic system of languages from Eastern Europe. Not until many years later, when I took a class in linguistics at Boise State University, did I understand why the Polish language came so easily to me. I learned that about eight Slavic languages are closely related to each other:

If a German, a Hungarian and a French person were stranded on a deserted island, it would take the group weeks or even months to be able to converse with each other. German, Hungarian and French are distinct and separate languages and it often takes years to master them.

If a Polish person, a Ukrainian and a Russian were stranded on a deserted island, it would take only a few days before they would be able to speak and function like one unit. This is because these three languages are dialects of one another. For years, I had wondered how I was able to learn a new language so quickly. After that class at Boise State University, I finally understood.

In my new home with Paul and Maria, I felt safe, loved and happy. It was like living in heaven. I had a nice home with a nice warm bed with plenty of food and no danger. Every day, Maria helped me with my bath and gave me some of her nice clothes to wear. All of her clothes were pretty although a bit too large for me. But I was so happy to wear them because they were hers.

One day, while Maria was washing my hair, she discovered that I had lice. I was embarrassed and humiliated beyond words. I was hoping she would never discover my shame. But Maria dried my hair and combed it over a large piece of white paper to show me that something had to be done. When I looked at the paper, there was no denying that I had a healthy population of lice.

Maria said to me in a kind voice, "You stay here while I go and ask my mother what to do." Soon she was back with a quart-size bottle of brown liquid. We applied this acrid smelling stuff to my hair and scalp every other morning for two weeks until all the lice and all their eggs were gone. I was so glad the biting and itching was over for good.

During the days when Paul was gone to work, Maria and I went to visit his parents or her parents every week. We often went to visit young couples who had children, especially small children. Maria and I would laugh and play with the babies and the children until it was time to go home to cook dinner for Paul. One day, on our way home, Maria told me that Paul and she could not have children. That is why they took me in. They wanted to help me and to love me as if I were their own.

Another Tragedy

Once in a while, Paul and Maria would quarrel late at night when they thought I was asleep. But in the morning, things seemed to be good again. Since I was afraid to ask any questions, I just quit worrying about them.

One day, when Paul was at work, Maria went down into the basement to do some work while I was doing embroidery upstairs. She came up several times to see if I was all right. Then she kissed me and said, "Do not go downstairs. I will be done with my project soon and then we will go to visit my mother." She knew I liked going to her parents' home.

Not long after Maria returned to the basement that last time, I heard a shot. I was not mistaken. It was a shot! I called Maria's name several times but she did not answer. Finally, with fear in my heart, I went downstairs. I found Maria lying on the floor. Her upper body was covered with blood and it was more than I could take. Blindly, I ran outside screaming. I wanted to get as far away from this tragedy as fast as I could go. I was hoping I was dreaming one of my terrible nightmares. I ran and screamed and screamed and screamed until our close neighbors saw me and came running to see what was wrong.

Paul was heartbroken and so were all his relatives, his brothers, his sisters and his close friends. They took me to Maria's parents' home since Maria's mother spoke some Ukrainian. Maria's parents were kind to me, overcoming their own grief and sorrow to help me understand what was going on.

They made sure to tell me that it was none of my fault. Maria's mother, whose name was Katya, was a kind person who gently comforted me in my own language.

Katya told me Maria had a very big problem but no one had been able to help her. "Paul tried," she said. "We all tried but no on could help her."

She said to me, "Don't worry, we will find you a safe home here in the village where we all will help you and see you often."

They all were so kind. To think that, in the face of their own grief, they were concerned about me long before I was able to worry about myself.

The funeral service at the little Catholic Church was long and beautiful. People of all ages and stations of life were there. It was clear that every one loved Maria dearly. Most had known her from her early childhood. Even though it was still early summer, the church was filled with beautiful home-grown flowers. But the service was so sad. It reminded me of my grandfather's funeral, which now seemed so long ago and so far removed from my present life.

The sadness was just as great at Maria's funeral as it had been at my grandfather's but the weather was warmer and gentler at Grajevo. The fierce cold had added to our suffering during my grandfather's funeral. I remembered and now wondered how my dear grandmother could have survived that day?

A week after Maria's funeral, Paul took me to meet a young family who were distant cousins of his. On the way there, he gave me his solemn promise that he would continue to search for my mother and, if he could, he would reunite us if that was what I wanted.

13. A New Home

My new home was a modest looking farm cottage not far from where Katya lived. This made me feel so much better.

I remember as if it were today; flowers were blooming everywhere while chickens, goats and dogs were busy doing what comes natural to them. There was a nice-looking garden to one side of the house and a small orchard on the other side.

A young couple stepped out as Paul knocked on the door. Paul said to me, "This is my cousin Lazlo and his wife Helena." Then, he said, "This is Lorissa; she is a bit scared and worried today but she is a brave little girl who has had a tough life so far."

Helena and Lazlo embraced me warmly and said, "Come and be our little girl! We have no children and you have no home; we will help and love each other."

Their home was not large but it was quite comfortable. There was a large living room, one bedroom for Lazlo and Helena and a good-sized kitchen. My little bed was all set up in a corner of the living room and ready for me to use it. A pretty partition, made by Lazlo and Helena, separated my corner from the rest of the room. Not far from the house, under a big tree, stood a neat and clean privy that was connected by a well-worn path with the cottage.

Paul brought in a box of things that Maria had given me and set it on the bed. Then, he said goodbye to everyone, gave me a kiss on my forehead and said, "Do not forget, I will be here to see you often." Then he left abruptly so no one would see his tears.

Helena and Lazlo's home was a noisy, happy place. They loved each other very much and showed it in every way possible, joking and playing with each other. As time went by, I, too, joined in their fun and frolic. Helena was a good cook and Lazlo was very proud of her cooking talents. Both of them worked on a large farm that was located not too far from their village. Lazlo worked six days a week and Helena worked part-time in the mornings five days a week.

They told me, "Do not go to the big farm; the Nazis come there often to check on our work and they might recognize you. We do not want them to take you away from us."

After a few days of adjustment, I was given a

few chores to do and that made me feel like a part of the family. I was to feed and water the chickens, gather the eggs and feed two goats. The two dogs were fed generous scraps from the table after each meal. It did not take me long to get my work done if I did not play with the animals. But I loved the animals. I loved the chickens and gathering the eggs was a special treat for me. The three goats were fun to feed, the young ones wanted to play while the pregnant mama-goat just wanted to be petted. The two dogs went with me everywhere.

Lazlo said to me, "No wonder the dogs are in love with you, you spoil them."

Helena and Lazlo were pleased with even the little I did to help them. On my own, in the mornings, I started to do the few dishes that were left in the kitchen. That pleased Helena very much. She said, "Nobody ever helped me in the kitchen until now."

In the evening, Helena milked one of the young goats. There was enough milk for us and for the elderly couple who lived in the next house down the road. Helena hugged and kissed me every day and I was eating it up like candy, maybe because Mother had hardly ever been affectionate with me. It was my grandmother who had supplied me with a generous number of hugs and kisses. I missed her loving kisses so much after we were separated.

The Bathhouse

As time went by, I met new people and learned about new places to go where it would be safe for me. One place I loved to go was the bathhouse. It was built on a small knoll overlooking the village.

Helena said, "There is hot water in the ground under the bathhouse. Since the hot water is free, it costs very little for people to bathe there."

The bathhouse was like a popular community center and going there was more fun than I had had since the war came to Kiev.

Our family went to the bathhouse every Saturday evening while the dogs waited for us outside. Inside, the building was divided into two sections, half for women and girls and the other half for men and boys. In each section, there was a huge shower room with dressing stalls all around the room. After the women and girls undressed, they gathered in the middle of the hot shower area. The women laughed and talked and scrubbed each other's backs while the little kids darted in and out from between our bare legs playing hide-and-go-seek. Nobody minded and nobody was bashful. Everyone was happy doing their own thing.

Every Saturday, two elderly ladies came to the

bathhouse carrying a bundle of dirty clothes under one arm and with the other hand carried a small round galvanized tub between them. Helena explained to me, "It is not allowed to wash clothes here but these old ladies seem to get away with it and nobody complains."

As soon as the old ladies undressed, they brought out their tub with the dirty garments already in it. Next, they set the tub directly under one of the hot shower heads and then stepped into the tub to soap and scrub themselves while all the hot soapy water collected in the tub with the dirty clothes. As the tub filled, the elderly ladies stomped and marched on the clothes; they became human washing machines. To tread and stomp like this was a difficult and tiring task for elderly ladies so these clever old women tried to entice the little girls to help them by stomping and running inside the tubs. At first, the kids thought it was great fun but that did not last long and the ladies were left to do their own work.

It was amazing how wonderful the hot mineral water felt. It was easy to overdo and stay longer than we intended until all our strength was sapped. After a half hour or so, our legs felt like rubber and we could hardly make it back home. Saturday nights we slept like logs.

As the weather became hotter and hotter, all the

young neighbors quit going to the bathhouse and instead went to the nearby river to swim and cool off, after which we had a community picnic supper. The first time I went, I said to Helena, "I do not have a swimming suit."

She laughed and said, "Do not worry."

As we were changing our clothes behind some big bushes, Helena pulled out of her big bag a red bathing suit just my size and said, "Here."

"Where did you get this," I asked with a surprise in my voice. She said with pride, "I made it from Lazlo's old red T-shirt."

I was amazed and so were all Helena's friends. I could hardly wait to put my new suit on and jump into the river. The water was cool and it felt so great; but when I stepped out of the river, the body of the wet swimsuit stretched so much that it hung around my waist and hips. The ladies took me aside and pinned up the suit to make it fit me better. It worked but Helena was disappointed that her efforts seemed to have failed. I, on the other hand, kept on swimming and having great fun.

After several months of living with Helena and Lazlo, I pretty much knew the routine of our home. Helena and I meshed well as we worked together. One morning, Lazlo appeared wearing the same kind of uniform that Paul had worn the day he took me from the *Straflager* (holding camp). I just sat at the table staring at him.

Lazlo looked uncomfortable and said in an apologetic tone, "I can't help it! We have to wear these uniforms when we deliver the produce from the farm to the holding camp. This way the Nazis know who we are and will let us in but, most importantly, they know to let us out."

To make me feel better, Lazlo said, "Now you have two of us, Paul and me, to see if we can find your mother."

Harsh Fate for Little Boy-Goat

One day Helena took me in her arms and said to me, "I have bad news for you. Remember I told you many weeks ago not to play with the young boy-goat? I know you love him best of all. Well, we have to butcher him this Saturday evening; we are out of meat."

For a moment, my heart stood still and I was blinded by my tears. I had suspected that this was coming but I could not help loving the little goat. He was so sweet, so playful and full of life. I knew butchering animals was part of farm life, Grandfather had taught me that a long time ago. Besides, Helena was so kind to me I could not make a big fuss about it. At my tender age, I understood so well about life and death on many different levels.

The next few weeks were pretty normal. By the first of June, the young goat was to be butchered.

I remember how Helena continued to milk the mama-goat and, in the afternoon, my job was to deliver a small jar of milk to the elderly couple who lived not far from us. The lady and her husband were quite old but they were so sweet. It was plain to see that they looked forward to my visit every evening. They always had a small treat for me. It was not much but it was special, an apple, a dried prune, a hand full of nuts, a pretty flower. . . .

To keep me from seeing the death of my sweet boy-goat, Helena made sure that I would spend the Saturday with our elderly neighbors.

It was early summer and the strawberries needed to be picked. Oh, the old folks thought they were so crafty. They worked hard all day to keep my mind occupied. But I could not think of anything else but what was going on at our cottage.

I helped cook our lunch and then we ate it leisurely in the shade of a big old tree. Later in the afternoon, I took down old family dishes from the high places in the kitchen and we washed them. After cleaning the shelves, I replaced the dishes.

It was a good day and the old folks had a good

time but I could not get my boy-goat out of my mind.

I thought of him and the other living beings in my life that had died. I wondered if I was the one who brought bad luck to everyone I came in contact? My grandfather had died, Olga had died after we befriended her, Maria had died after I came to live with them and now my boy-goat had died after I came to live with Helena and Laszlo. My heart was heavy that afternoon and waves of guilt washed over me all day long.

By evening, I knew that my sweet boy-goat was gone forever and it was time for me to go home. With a dish of ripe strawberries for Helena and Lazlo, I headed out with a heavy heart.

When I arrived home, everything seemed normal except that the kitchen floor was freshly scrubbed; that was where they butchered his body. Helena and Lazlo were gone but I did not worry. They never went too far without me. Soon they were back. They looked tired and dirty but happy; happiness was their usual state of being.

Life in Grajevo

The people of Grajevo were forced to make many compromises in order to survive war, just as my people in Kiev did. But the Polish people here were lucky to be living near a huge formerly Communist collective farm. I was told that people from the surrounding villages had been forced to work on this farm all their lives; they did not know anything different. What the Communists did not take when they retreated, the Nazis used to operate the farm and feed their own army. The people in the villages, including ours, were needed to do the farm work and so were valuable to the Nazis. Because of that, they were spared the kind of horrors that the people of Kiev had had to endure.

The summer turned into fall and with it came new activities. I asked about attending the village school but Helena said, "It would be too dangerous this year, the Nazis might be checking the registration records." Then, she said, "But I hope by next year it will be safer or maybe the war will be over."

We picked apples and dug potatoes and stored them in the fruit cellar for the winter. That reminded me of our frozen potatoes in Kiev and how our family had faced sure starvation that terrible winter.

Lazlo and Helena and I went into the woods not far from the village on a wagon pulled by two young donkeys to get wood for the winter. The cart and the two donkeys belonged to the village, a collective ownership patterned after the Communist concept.

Lazlo said, "This weekend, it was our turn to get the wood. Later this winter, we can use the cart and donkeys again but for now we will gather enough wood to last us until after New Year's and maybe a little longer."

Everything we did together was fun. Helena made special foods for us to eat and Lazlo was good at playing a clown while we worked and laughed all day long. In the evening, even though we were tired, we were happy that we had plenty of wood to last us through most of the winter. Again, I was reminded of the fence that had been stolen and the antique furniture that Grandfather had had to chop up for wood. I could still hear Grandmother's sad whimpers for the loss of her family heirlooms and their wedding gift.

Christmas was a collective affair in Grajevo. All the people of the village gathered in an old community house to eat, drink, sing and dance. There were no presents but nobody missed them. I remembered the last Christmas Grandfather was still alive and the white cap and mittens trimmed in red that our neighbor, Rosa, had made for me. My new friends were happy just to be alive and I was their reminder of how bad things could have been for them if they had been in my place.

Paul Finds Mother

Sometime in late January of 1944, Paul came to see us. After we ate, we all sat at the table and by the candlelight Paul told me that my mother was back in the camp.

He said, "Your mother is very thin but she is well. So far, I have had no chance to talk with her but I saw her every time last week when I delivered the produce to the camp. She is working in the kitchen and that is good because she will get a little more to eat. One day, I will be able to talk to her. Do you remember the young woman who wears the same uniform as we do, who can speak Ukrainian and who works in the camp? When the time is right, she will tell your mother about you, that you are alive and well. Later, we will decide what to do."

Poor Helena, all the while Paul was talking, she was crying. I was glad to hear that Mother was alive and well but I had mixed feelings. I wanted to be with my mother but I knew that Helena would be deeply hurt and I would miss living with her and Lazlo. I did not want to go back to the holding camp knowing that, sooner or later, I would be facing death like everyone else. I knew that, living in the camp, any of us could be killed at any moment by the Nazis.

Before Paul left, he said, "As soon as I have any news I will come to have supper with you."

By mid-May, I had become very sick. I had the same old high fever with sore throat and a deep pain in my chest. The constant coughing was so severe that it caused me to wet my pants. For over a week, my life hung in the balance between life and death.

I knew that Helena stayed home to care for me. She cooled my high fever with wet towels and kept plenty of water and milk at my bedside. There were no doctors in Grajevo during the war. Helena depended on her mother's extensive knowledge about folk medicine and her good advice.

Helena told me how, late one evening, I woke up in a feverish panic to plead with God, "Please, God, do not let me die. Please, God, let me live!" After that, my fever broke and I started on the road to recovery.

Helena said, "You were a very sick girl. You had a bad case of chicken pox and we thought we would lose you. Thank God we still have you."

While I was ill, I lost my appetite and all I wanted was water and some milk. I had lost a lot of weight.

By the end of May, Paul had come to have supper with us again. He said to me, "I spoke with your mother and she knows you are alive and well. She sends her best wishes to you. We must wait until you regain some weight and become stronger before we take you back if you still want to go."

A month after this meeting, Paul arrived at our house late one night. He looked concerned. He said, "There will be a train leaving for Germany from the camp in few days. No one knows who will be on the train and no one knows where the train is going. It could be to a work camp or it could be to a concentration camp. This is not a good time to reunite you with your mother. We do not know, she might be leaving on the train. Let us wait and hope for the best."

I could see Helena was relieved when she heard this news. She was hoping against all hope that I would stay with them. I, too, had mixed feelings about leaving the village and facing the unspeakable hardships and fear of the unknown.

Before Paul left that night he said, "I think it will be a couple of weeks or maybe longer before it will be safe to try, if that is still your decision." Then he handed me a burlap sack and said, "You can open it after I am gone. Maybe, you will need these things later."

I could hardly wait to see what was in the sack. It turned out to be all my old clothes that I had been wearing the day Paul brought me to his home. The clothes had been washed, mended and neatly folded. The underwear and my long home-knitted stockings had been replaced with new ones. Among my old things, I found my white cap and mittens trimmed in red that Rosa had knitted for me as a Christmas gift. I remembered how unexpected that gift was in the days of extreme hardship and danger. My old worn-out shoes had been repaired and scuffed up so that they would look old and worn-out.

Helena was at my side as I went through my old things. Tearfully, she told me that Paul's mother had washed, mended and replaced the worn-out things to the best of her ability. She added, "But Katya hoped that you would never need to use these things again, that you would stay here with us in the village."

For a long time, Helena and I sat on the floor holding each other and crying. It was heartbreaking for both of us and I did not know what to do; this life-altering decision was solely mine to make.

A Difficult Dilemma

I could not stop thinking about this dilemma. I saw myself being pulled in three different directions: Helena loved me as her own child. Her heart was breaking at the thought of losing me. I knew my mother needed me more than anyone else. And I kept hearing my grandfather's voice reminding me about family loyalty and love for my mother who had given me life.

As for myself, I did not want to give up my safe home and the happy life that fate had handed me. But I wanted to do the right thing by Mother and Helena. All through my illness, as I lay in a feverish coma, I kept worrying about my dilemma that seemed to have no solution.

I had feelings of loyalty and love for my mother. I had love and gratitude for Helena. Helena and Lazlo accepted me into their home and gave me a second chance after Maria was gone. In Grajevo, I felt safe and my life was getting back to normal, the way it was in Kiev before the occupation. Yes, I did see trucks full of Nazi soldiers drive through the village but they were not looking for me or stopping to capture people. They were on their way to oversee the farm production and the delivery of food to the *Straflager* and to the trains that regularly went to the frontlines where the war was being fought.

In my desperation, my thoughts turned to my grandparents. I thought of my loving grandmother and my wonderful grandfather and of their love for each other and the many sacrifices they made for their family. They loved my mother and they loved me because we were their flesh and blood. For the first time, I could see what it meant to be a part of a strong and loving family.

Grandfather had taught us that family was very important to my grandparents and it should be important to me. Grandfather had taught us that love and loyalty was an expression of close family ties. That thought convinced me that my place was by my mother's side. Living a good life and feeling safe was not as important to me as being with my mother who needed me and my support right now.

The next time Paul asked me about my decision, "Are you sure about this?" I would answer without reservation, "Yes, I am sure."

The Months of Waiting

In the early evening during the summer, we went swimming and on Saturday, we went to the bathhouse. Helena and I picked more berries to make jam that was as good as my grandmother's jam. We took a jar to the elderly couple. I think they knew all about the hard decision I had made. The lady hugged me in a tender and loving way and the whole village acted the same way. It was difficult to face them and keep a smile on my face when my tears were so ready to flow. But I was glad that the decision was behind me; I would accept whatever was to come.

The hot summer turned into early fall and Paul still had no news for me. He told me that mid-fall would be the best time for us to make the move. It was dangerous to do what we had in mind. If we were caught, Paul and all the people in the village as well as Mother and I would be in mortal danger.

And so, life kept moving on. We were happy being busy during the day and, at night, we rested. But the early-fall nights were long and boring. There were no books to read, no Grandfather to tell us his wonderful stories.

Often at night, it fell on me to tell the others what I had learned from my grandfather so long ago. I told them what we went through during the Nazi occupation in Kiev. In no time, friends and relatives came over in the evening and stayed late into the night just to listen to a ten-year-old girl tell stories.

All of us would sit in the cool dark outside and it was up to me to become my grandfather. Helena often prompted me about some of the stories I had already told her and Lazlo. Of course, Grandfather's wolf story was the one everyone liked the best. After all, Grajevo was surrounded by thick, dark forest and even though the wolves were extinct in this area, the people could easily relate to what Grandfather had gone through.

I also told them how, for lack of food, people in

Kiev were reduced to eating horseflesh, how Grandfather chopped up Grandmother's priceless antique furniture for firewood, how Mother and Grandmother, all by themselves, prepared Grandfather's body for the funeral, how a young Nazi soldier killed Olga's grandfather at the market. I told them how Olga and seven other teenage girls were taken off the train and how the train went on without them, how the heartbroken mothers screamed and beat their heads against the cattle car doors in their grief. The women listening to my story cried and even the men were deeply touched.

I told of how we were randomly gathered up in the marketplace and forced into trucks and then into cattle cars, and how we finally arrived at the holding camp in Poland. These stories were a simple outpouring of my sorrowing heart and they made the people of the Grajevo realize how lucky they were. Through my sad but true stories, they came to know me better. I became their brave little Ukrainian girl. Many of them said, "You are a little girl of ten but you tell stories like a woman your mother's age."

During one of those evenings, some men were passing news around in secretive whispers: America (that was the first time I heard the word 'America') had entered the war on the side of Russia, England and all the other countries that were now under Nazi control. Every day they were bombing Germany.

The villagers said, "Now we have hope! Every day we must pray to our Holy Mother and her Son, Jesus Christ (most Polish people are Catholic) that maybe soon we will be set free."

Go With God, My Brave Little Girl

I remember that sunny golden fall of 1944 in Poland. It was beautiful but eventually the rains came and came and came . . . . The days became shorter and the cold weather slowly crept in. I knew that soon Paul would be coming to say, "It is time for us to make the move."

And so it was. One evening, Paul was at our door with a sad face and a heavy heart. Without making eye contact with us, he said, "Early tomorrow morning, about 5 o'clock, we must be ready to go. Do you still want to go? If yes, are you ready?"

I answered, "Yes!" to all his questions.

During the dinner, Paul said, "I am so glad we had you in our home and you will stay in our hearts forever. Maria wanted a child more than life itself and I was desperate to help her. When I saw you all alone standing by the gate, I knew this was our one and only chance to have a child. I pulled you into the cab of the truck and you did not resist me. All I remember was your tear-stained dirty face and your sad blue eyes. At that moment, I knew I did the right thing for you and for us. But later, I felt guilty for the pain I caused your mother. I did not think she would be back. Usually, when the Nazis took some-one from the camp, they were never seen again."

Then Paul explained to me, "Now we have a big problem. How do I get you into the camp without being caught? There are new soldiers and new com-manders in the camp and we think this will make it easier for you to blend in. You must not talk to anyone. Keep your head down and keep busy doing your work. When you meet your mother, be calm and quiet, as if you saw her every day. Your mother knows what to do and she will help you."

Paul continued, "Tonight we must say our good-byes; in the morning, there will be no time for hugs and kisses and tears. Do not forget, Lorissa, wear your old clothes and don't forget to smear a little dirt on your face, neck and hands. Do not comb your hair; you must look like the rest of the people in the camp."

To say 'good-bye' was more difficult than I had ever thought it would be. Helena was crying, La-zlo and Paul were sobbing and I stood in the midst of them also sobbing with a broken heart. After a while, Paul left and, in order to calm Helena down, I crawled in bed with her and Lazlo. We did not sleep that night but clung to each other as if for dear life.

I can still hear Helena asking, "Why do you have to go? We love you so much." She repeated this over and over again.

In the morning, Helena was getting breakfast ready for us while I was getting dressed in my little corner by my comfortable little bed. I sat on the floor with the bag of my old clothes scattered out before me. I was crying so hard it was difficult to see what I was doing. The night before, Helena and I had been concerned that after more than a year, the clothing might be too small for me. But in the morning, I found that everything still seemed to fit.

We all were too upset to eat that morning. Helena was quiet and Lazlo was worried about our safety. We hugged each other for the last time and kissed good-bye. Helena kissed me again and said, "Go with God, our brave little girl!"

I had never heard that expression before but I remember it to this day. From that day on, that phrase was lodged in my mind. Every time I faced danger and there were many dangers to face—I said to myself, "Go with God, brave little girl!"

In retrospect, I can see how very dangerous our situation was. At any moment, the Nazi soldiers could become suspicious and kill us in a blink of an eye. But death was no longer a stranger to me.

That morning, I stepped out forever from a world I had come to know and away from people I would love for the rest of my life.

14. Return to the Straflager

It was still dark when Paul, Lazlo and I, in that order, got into the pickup. On the way to the camp, Paul told me, "When we drive up to the gate, you must crouch down on the floor between Lazlo's legs. After we are past the checkpoint, we will drive to the kitchen building where your mother is working. The door to the kitchen will be across from the pickup. I will pick up a large box to carry inside. Then you will jump out behind me and slowly walk to the door as if you have done this many times before. Your mother will be inside to tell you what to do. But remember, do not show any sign of fear or joy."

Everything worked out the way Paul had planned. Inside the kitchen, there were six busy people and Mother working at a large table cutting up vegetables and other foods. When Mother saw me, she casually came up to me and, without saying a word, handed me a broom and a dustpan. She pointed to the cluttered mess on the floor but especially under the table. In a bossy manner, Mother said, "Sweep up the mess and do a good job!"

I was so glad to hear her voice and to see her face. My heart was beating fast with joy but all I could do was look into her eyes and see the sorrow and pain that was there. I wanted to hug her but I knew that our lives depended on both of us acting as if we hardly knew and certainly did not care about each other.

After our day of work was done, I followed mother to the barracks. At once, we went to bed next to each other but only after the lights were out did we hug and hold each other with gladness in our hearts. Mother whispered, "When we are alone we can talk a little at a time so no one will become suspicious of us."

There came a day when most of the inmates in the camp were loaded into the cattle cars again and shipped to Germany. Most everyone, except for the kitchen crew, were gone. We were told to clean the kitchen from top to bottom and get ready for the next large shipment of people to arrive soon. We were in the kitchen for days scrubbing the floors, scouring the tables and washing the walls and the windows.

A Chance to Talk

During the downtime, Mother and I had a chance to be apart from the others as we worked in a small storage room sorting potatoes. We shared our experiences and silently cried while hugging each other. Much had happened to each of us in the past eighteen months. My story was a happy one compared to what Mother had to tell me when her turn came.

I told Mother how Paul had stolen me from the *Straflager* to be his and Maria's little girl. I told her, "He knew that you were gone from the camp and, from his past experience, he knew that those who were taken from the camp were never seen again. All Paul wanted to do was help a poor little girl who was wandering aimlessly looking for her mother and to give his broken-hearted barren wife a child to love."

I told Mother all about the little village, the kind people and the two young families with whom I had lived for all those months. With a heavy heart, I told Mother how Maria had committed suicide within the first two months of my stay with them and how Paul, despite his own sorrow, was so concerned about me. I told her of how Paul had found me another home with a loving family who wanted and needed a child to love. I told mother all about

Maria and Paul and their love for each other. I also told her about Helena and Lazlo, how they loved me from the first day they saw me, how heartbroken they were when I decided to leave them and come to be by her side no matter what would happen to us in the future.

Mother said, "You have grown up to be a wise daughter and a pretty young girl." But she was concerned about my good looks.

She said, "You are too young to hear what I have to say to you but I must tell you for your own good. German guards are going crazy these days. Many of their officers are gone and the discipline is very lax. They know they are losing the war and they are worried for their own lives. They drink too much and they chase women after dark every night."

Mother stopped to wipe her tears, then she went on, "They hate all of us and call us all sorts of terrible names but, after dark, they rape our women and girls if they can catch them."

Mother went on to say, "You must not wash yourself, especially your face. Make yourself smell bad. Don't wash or comb your hair. Your hair is long and pretty but I will cut it off to make it look ugly. Above all, keep your head down and don't look into their eyes. After dark, stay in the barracks and do not use the privy at night if you can wait till morning."

There were no mirrors in the camp. I did not know what I looked like but I saw myself in the faces of others. I saw dirty faces with sunken cheeks, deep-set frightened eyes and defeated expressions. We were gaunt and our loose clothing hung on us and made us look like scarecrows. We moved on stiff legs as if we were the walking dead.

As an afterthought, Mother said, "Last summer we had a bad outbreak of typhoid in this camp. Many people came down with the fever and died. The Nazis placed the sick people in the small building not far from the gate. Most of them died there but a few younger ones survived."

Mother went on to say, "I am glad you were not here last summer to see what we went through. At night, the Nazis made us carry out and bury the dead before the flies could spread the disease. Not long before you returned to the camp, the Nazis declared that the disease was over."

Mother's Ordeal

When it was Mother's turn to tell me her story, she said, "When the Gestapo came to get me they also took the old Jewish couple with them. We did not go very far until we came to a two-story brick house in the middle of a field. The first night, they

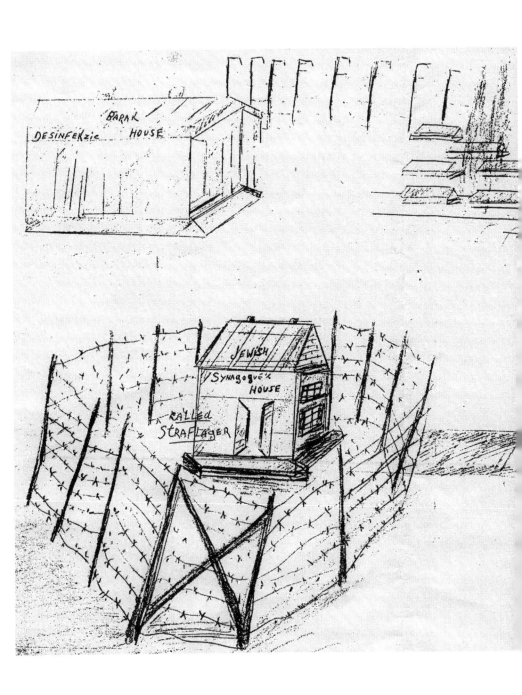

Another of Mother's sketches made after she came to America. She carried vivid, dark memories of our captivity in the holding camp at Grajevo and the concentration camp at Dachau.

put us in a cold dirty room in the basement, an empty coal bin. Before they left us, they told us to undress and give them our clothing. We sat huddling in a corner on the cold cement floor all night long and part of the next morning."

Mother continued, "When the Nazis came down the stairs, they were drunk. With their thundering footsteps and boisterous voices, they let us know that we were facing serious trouble. The Nazis were arguing with each other but we could not understand what was going on. Finally, the soldiers told the Jewish couple, '*Komm, mach schnell*' (Come quickly). The old couple started to wail pitifully but there was no one there to help them. The Gestapo had no pity in their hearts for the elderly couple. They were a sorry sight as they stumbled up the stairs on their stiff old legs. Their naked bodies were wrinkled from age and black from coal dust. They could hardly climb the stairs. The ruthless Nazi guards were poking them with their quirts and bayonets in their private parts and the old couple tripped and fell while begging for mercy . . . . All the while, the Nazi Gestapo laughed like hyenas."

"Oh, how I hated them," Mother said bitterly.

"After they were outside," she continued, "it was not long before I heard many guns go off. Over and over again rang out the rat-tat-tat of the guns. It was a frightful sound but I knew the old couple was not suffering anymore. Then, for the rest of the day, it was silence."

Mother paused for a moment and then resumed her story. "Next morning they came down for me. Cold and hungry, I stood naked before a group of young Nazi men. They were asking me many questions but I did not understand them. So, back to the black hole they sent me but, this time, they gave me my clothes and a bowl of hot soup.

Next day, when I was brought up, there was a young Polish girl who spoke broken Ukrainian and German. This time, I was able to understand what was wanted of me. They wanted to know if I was a daughter of the old Jewish couple. Was I Jewish? Was I a spy for the Communist Army? And many more questions. I answered all those questions in the negative. But they were not satisfied. According to the Gestapo, this called for drastic measures. They had torture in mind.

"From that day on, I was brought up and tortured in a savage way. They beat me on my back and on my head with the butts of their pistols. During the first torture, my lower teeth were knocked out and my back injured until I could hardly walk. The torture continued for days. The Nazis brought in other people to torture and for a few days the Gestapo was busy with this new group. But before long, it was my turn again. The Gestapo placed me over a stool on my stomach and beat me with their guns until I bled from my nose and my mouth. They interrogated me for long periods of time. If they were dissatisfied with the results, they would call me a Ukrainian swine-dog. After all that, I could not walk to the basement so they helped me by pushing me down the stairs."

Hellhole

Mother continued telling me her story. "One day, two Gestapo came down to ask me if I could cook. They knew I could cook; I had told them so during the interrogations. Yes, I can cook, I said. The Nazis made clear to me that if I lied and did not cook well, I would be shot. Then, all at once and quite unexpectedly, I was moved from the basement to the first floor. I had a nice warm room. The Nazis had the best meat and vegetables for me to cook and I tried my best to please them. I knew my life depended on my cooking abilities. If I did well, I might live a little longer but there were no guarantees.

"All that time, I did not know what had happened to you. Since I was allowed to live close to the kitchen on the first floor, I kept looking for you but with no luck. The Nazis never talked to me about you, as if they did not know I had a child, and I was afraid to ask. One day, a young Polish woman who spoke Ukrainian came to the kitchen to ask for a glass of water. While I was getting her a glass, she told me in a whisper that you were alive and living in a nearby village called Grajevo. After hearing this, my heart was full of hope. I was beside myself with anticipation of seeing you but I was told not to share my good news with anyone. Before this, my blackest thoughts had convinced me that you were dead. The news about you was a miracle to me!

"The Gestapo who ate my food with relish had been nice to me but I could not trust them to ask for help. I knew, instead of helping, they would turn their guns on you and me."

A Hard Winter and Illness

Soon after I arrived back in the camp to be with Mother, the weather turned freezing cold. Snow and wind blew in from the large fields surrounding our camp, depositing snowdrifts everywhere. The wind whistled and blew from one corner of the camp to the other. The kitchen crew felt lucky they did not have to work outside since nobody's clothing was adequate for this kind of weather.

A large load of Ukrainians was delivered to the camp, but this time the people did not seem as downcast as the previous groups had been. At night, when it was safe, they shared their good news in guarded whispers. They said, "The Nazis are losing their grip on the war. They have already retreated from Russia, Ukraine and now they are retreating from other parts of Europe."

They said, "The Americans have a strong army and many fast modern planes. When they fly over-head in huge formations, you can hear them in the sky and feel the earth tremble and shake. But all we can do right now is pray, be brave and wait. Finally, God and America are on our side! If we live long enough, we will be free."

Things were going well until December of 1944 when I came down with a severe bladder infection. Without a doctor or any medication, I suffered se-verely and my healing process was slow and pain-ful. At night, because of urinary urgency, I could not sleep. I was up and down, running to the privy.

The communal privy was a long ditch covered with a low-hung roof and no walls. The Nazis want-ed to see us day and night; we had no privacy. There was one privy for men and one for women. The peo-ple sat on the pole side by side, over a deep ditch; toilet paper was unheard of at the camp.

Sitting on the pole, while the freezing wind blasted past my feverish unclad bottom, was more than I could bear. I dribbled the urine slowly while the burning pain brought tears to my eyes. Then back to bed, only to get up and run again. I did not dare cry out with pain and had to bite my lower lip and let my tears flow in silence. It was well known in the camp that sick inmates were segregated and eventually destroyed like dogs.

Mother was beside herself with her desire to help me but she did not know what to do. In desperation, she decided to fill a glass bottle with hot water from the kitchen and carry it hidden under her coat to the barracks. At night, the hot-water bottle was a godsend for me. I kept it on my lower abdomen as long as it stayed warm. With that came relief and with relief came sleep. It took a long time for me to heal but, eventually, I got well and the Nazis never discovered my secret.

In early January of 1944, I developed a painful infection in my right eye. My body must have been so drained that my immune system was at its lowest point. Otherwise, why would I be sick more often than anyone else I knew? The weather was still cold and there was still snow on the ground. When the sun shone, the bright light reflecting off the snow caused me great pain.

Again, I had to suffer in secret. No matter how hard I tried to cover up my right eye, the stubborn sun rays penetrated through my fingers and caused me piercing pain. When I moved my left eye in any direction, it caused my right eye to suffer. Tears and pain were my constant companions as my eye slowly began to heal.

By mid-February, I was back to normal and mother said, "*Slavo Bogu!*" (Praise God! in Russian) you are well and let us pray that you will stay that way."

New Inmates Bring News

I remember how every time a new group of inmates was brought into the camp, we were anxious to hear any news they might have from the outside world. In the winter of 1944-1945, the big news was that the Germans were retreating from the countries formerly occupied by the fierce Nazis. This news was unbelievable to us; the Nazis were so strong, so numerous and so ruthless that we felt dominated and resigned to our own death and the destruction of our race.

Some of our fellows now said, "We have them on the run." We learned that Kiev had been recaptured by the Red Army and that brought tears of joy to our eyes. Germany was being bombed and, by now, many German cities lay in ruins. We heard how the city of Dresden, with all the factories that made world famous china, had been leveled.

We were told, "In many parts of Germany, you can hear and feel American air power as their planes fly overhead on their missions. Stay strong; soon we will be liberated."

It was being whispered that the Nazis were beginning to close down the work camps and that they were loading the looted treasures onto military trucks and trains and sending that loot to Germany.

It was not long before other news was being circulated. The gossip of the day was that our camp would soon be closing and all the people sent to Germany. This news struck terror in our hearts. We did not know whether we would be shipped to a work camp or to one of the infamous concentration camps that were located in many parts of Germany.

We had known for a long time that although our holding camp was not a picnic, it was much safer than the concentration camps in Germany. In here, we died from cold, prolonged hunger and overwork but we were not being exterminated. Now, we were hearing of places like Auschwitz, with its gas chambers, the most feared concentration camp of all. Treblinka was the most inhumane camp in Poland and

Dachau was one of the worst camps in Germany.

When told we might be moved, Mother turned deathly pale. I saw terror in her wide-open eyes. She cried out, "Oh my God! Oh my God! I thought we might be saved in the holding camp but now, it seems we are doomed. All our hopes are gone."

When we heard about the grim fate that might be awaiting us, Mother and I clung to each other and the silent tears that ran down our faces mingled as if they flowed from one heart breaking with sorrow.

During these difficult times, Mother often said to me, "Just keep focusing on the future that is the only hope we have. For now, we are forced to live in the present and that is not a safe place to be."

Often, when everything looked the darkest, I retreated into the past and my memories of when my grandfather was alive and when there was love, joy and safety in our home. In my mind, I asked Grandfather, What happened to the universal code you told me about so long ago? When all men were born with a sense of right and wrong? What about the Nazis? Where is their sense of right and wrong? As far as I can see, they only know how to deliver death and evil. But my grandfather was dead. There was no one to answer my questions or to comfort me in my time of need.

Part Three
Concentration Camp

gas
chamber

212   I Remember . . .

15. A Boxcar Ride to Hell

I remember that on the last morning in the *Straflager* in Poland, everyone was on edge. Fear was so strong, I could taste it. We were worried about what we would be facing. When first we were brought to this holding camp, we thought it was the worst place on earth. But now, we were reluctant to leave it, dreading to face the horrors of our new destination. The holding camp seemed safe compared to where we were going. It was well known that the holding camps were revolving doors to other concentration camps where the inmates were gassed and cremated. No matter how we looked at it, our future appeared grim.

There was a sense of urgency in the air. The rumors persisted that the Germans were losing the war. That was why the officers and soldiers were frantically trying to clear out the camp and retreat behind their own lines as fast as possible. The Nazi guards were busy putting everything in order with typical

German precision. During the previous few months, they had burned records and lists and packed away other things in big boxes to go.

Then, one morning, we were told to get ready to leave but we had nothing to get ready except what was on our backs. To our surprise, at the last minute, we were told to bring our blankets along. For this we were grateful because it was December 1944 and the weather was damp and blustery.

In the afternoon, we were told to line up in a column. We had to stand in line for hours while the guards searched every barracks to make sure no one was hiding in the dark recesses of the empty buildings. Finally, the guards were satisfied. They and their dogs were positioned on each side of our pitiful human column and we were ordered to march!

When we arrived at the railroad tracks, instead of cattle cars, I saw a line of boxcars. The leading half-dozen of the boxcars were uncovered and already filled with inmates from other camps. The rest of the boxcars were covered. Again, we were told to stop and wait.

There was an eerie silence in the air except for the stomp, stomp of our worn-out boots on the muddy road as we tried to keep our feet warm. By now, most of our footwear was falling apart. Some of our boots were being held together by remnants of belts, old twine and rusted wire found along the road. My feet had grown so much during the few last months that my bare toes were sticking out of my boots. My feet were numb with cold. I had no socks and neither did anyone else. Our socks, gloves, caps and underwear had rotted off our bodies long ago.

As we stood waiting, the rain turned into sleet; we were getting wetter and colder by the minute. Someone in the column said, "These blankets are getting wet and making us colder rather than warmer."

Some one else said, "The blankets are heavy with water and with the weight of the thousands of lice that live there."

Everyone burst out laughing. Our hysterical laughter was a welcome release from a terrible tension that we were feeling.

I remember how in response to our laughter, the Nazi guards raised their guns to their shoulders. They were ready to kill us right then. When Nazi army began to lose the war and the American bombers flew over Germany without resistance, the Nazi guards became sensitive to everything we said and did. They now seemed to be afraid even of us and of what we might have to say. For the first time, we saw fear in their eyes as they shook their fists in rage at the American planes overhead.

Secretly, we enjoyed every small sign of pain and fear that we saw in them. We felt like saying, "Take that and that, you bloodthirsty brutes!" But we had to be very careful since desperate men are prone to take drastic actions and the Nazis only knew how to kill and destroy. From then on, we were more careful.

Everyone was wondering what was going on. What would happen to us next? We knew we could not last much longer. Our physical strength and our mental resolve to survive had been depleted to the point of no return. Ever since we had come in contact with the Nazi forces in Kiev, each day had brought us closer to death and now, we felt as if we were close to the end.

The Nazi guards separated us into the groups of eighty. Then they chose one person in each group to be accountable for the rest of the people. A Nazi soldier who knew Mother worked in the kitchen chose her as the ill-fated person to be in charge of one group. Then he chose two other women to be in charge of the other two groups of eighty.

He said to the three women, "You must be responsible for your own group. If one person in your group disappears, you will be shot like a dog.

The Nazi guard smiled at Mother sadistically. He pointed to three large burlap sacks of bread and four large buckets of water and said, "This evening, divide the bread chunks evenly among the people and each morning give everyone a cup of water."

Mother looked helplessly at the Nazi soldier with hollow lifeless eyes, slowly nodded her head in an agreement and said, "Yah."

Before we were allowed to climb into the boxcars, a Nazi officer came up with a large box and said, "This will be your last chance to surrender your valuables. Anyone who does not comply will be shot."

As the officer walked among our group, he collected several gold rings, a few silver neck chains and a couple of watches. But the officer was unhappy with his meager collection. He kept walking among us, waving his pistol and saying, "You better do it now."

But no one had anything more to give. Besides, we had been threatened by the Nazis so many times by now that the threat of death rang hollow in our ears. We knew they could kill us any moment and there was nothing we could do about it. No amount of gold or any number of valuables could save our live

At dusk, we were loaded into the boxcars, soaked, freezing and hungry. At least the boxcars did not reek of manure and there were no big chunks of cow dung to stumble over. At least the floor was clean but we missed the straw that we had in Kiev. There was no hole in the corner of the floor to be used as a toilet and this was a problem that Mother would have to solve later. When she asked if anyone had a knife, everyone laughed. She knew that no one was allowed to possess any kind of sharp weapon. If a weapon was found on an inmate, it was a sure death sentence. It was clear that there were no tools that could be used to make a hole in the floor.

As soon as the boxcar doors slid shut and the lock clicked, we felt trapped. In the dark of the night, we felt cut off from the rest of the world. We were lost souls and we knew that no one cared about us. In silence, each one of us was agonizing over our present state of being. We knew that our final voyage toward death had begun. But where were they taking us? Would it be Auschwitz, Treblinka, Sobibor or Dachau? There was no good choice.

Shortly after the train began to move, Mother and the other ladies started to organize their groups. They said, "We want to hand out the bread as soon as possible! We know you are cold and hungry. The bread in your stomachs will help you to warm up. Remember, we do not know how long we will be locked up in this boxcar. Do not eat your bread all at once! If you do, later on you will be sorry! We do not know how many pieces of bread we have so please stand up and line up around the boxcar. We will give each of you two chunks of bread until everyone is served. If there is any bread left over, then we will decide how to divide it."

Unexpectedly, Mother said in a loud voice, so everyone could hear her, "Lorissa, will you take four chunks of bread to the sick lady and her son and we will start giving out bread to the people in line. You will be at the end of the line."

When all the bread had been given out, there was very little bread and just a few crumbs left. Mother and the other ladies decided to give the leftover bread and crumbs to those who were the weakest. To Mother's surprise, no one objected. As a rule, the inmates fought over every crumb of bread or apple-core that fell on the ground. Once a Nazi guard discarded a half-eaten apple and when he saw that I was looking at it, he stomped on it and ground it into dirt with his boot.

The people in our boxcar knew Mother well because she had worked in the kitchen. She was the one who served the food to them twice a day. People often said to me, "Your mother is a fair and good woman. She cared for all and always stirred the soup so that everyone got something besides watery soup in their cup. She was good to us."

The train pushed on for most of the night. After we ate our bread, we warmed up a little and as we lay close to each other, we felt better. We all were so used to the stench of our own and others' bodies that we did not notice how badly we smelled. But the Nazi soldiers always yelled at us to stay away from them. They said, "You are pigs. You stink and you are dirty."

Mother said to me, "That is fine with us. You stay dirty and you smell bad and they will leave you alone. Remember, dirt and stink is your protection."

Finally, with the rhythmic clickaty-clack, clickaty-clack of the wheels on the tracks, we were lulled into sleep. But before we fell asleep, Mother whispered to me, "One day soon when we are alone, I need to talk to you. It is important." She had said this to me several times before but we could not find a time to be alone.

During the night, I woke up with what I thought was a mild toothache. But it turned out to be a humming in my head. The humming turned into a strong vibration. By then, others were awake. They were listening and talking with excitement. With joy, they identified the strong-vibration that shook our boxcar as a fleet of American bombers.

Someone said, "Americans are on their way to

destroy the Nazi war machine." We clenched our fists and yelled like wild animals with jubilation. Nothing could have warmed us up faster then our own loud outbursts of pure joy. Our long-suppressed hate for our vile captors exploded within us like fireworks. For the first time, we heard the bombing and, saw through the cracks in the boxcar's walls, the lights flashing in the distance as the Nazi artillery tried to protect what was left of their munitions factories. Every time a bomb exploded, we cheered. We did not care if we were heard. We were willing to perish with the bombing as long as the Nazis perished with us.

In the morning, the train was still moving. Mother said to the group, "I think I solved the toilet problem. After we each drink a cup of water, we will have at least one empty bucket."

Upon hearing Mother's solution, there was a great relief on our faces and everyone clapped. As it turned out, we used up almost two buckets of water. Mother topped off the other two pails to free up the second container. The people decided that even though we might perish soon, we did not want to live like animals. While someone was using the 'toilet', two or three people would stand in front of the pail to create a human privacy screen. That worked well and gave us a great sense of dignity.

Mother said, "Our bodies are void of food and water, we are empty. Whatever we ate and drank in the past few days has been assimilated by our starved bodies and these two pails should be enough to hold all our waste." As it turned out, Mother was right.

Sometime during the second night, the sick lady died but we did not discover it until the next morning. Her little son was snuggled next to her body for warmth and comfort and would not let go of her.

Some said, "He does not realize she is dead. She was a brave lady who suffered in silence mostly for the sake of her son."

It was hard to tell how old the woman was since hard work and starvation had aged her beyond her true age. Someone who knew her from pre-war times said, "She was a beautiful young woman and a good mother to her three children." No one knew what had happened to her other children and her son was not able to talk.

Even though we were strangers thrown together by our cruel fate, we shared a deep sorrow for the loss of the boy's mother. The child was inconsolable, silently crying. Many women in the boxcar tried to comfort him but he wanted to be left alone. In the end, the boy chose to sleep next to Mother and me. My heart went out to him. I knew how it felt to lose a loved one. His ordeal reminded me of the day I saw and touched my grandfather in his casket. Mother and I tried to comfort him as best we could.

By the end of the third day, our bread was gone and we had very little water left. In a sense, I was glad my second piece of bread was gone. I had eaten the first piece right away but the second piece burned a hole in my pocket for quite a while. As long as I had that second piece of bread, I had no peace. I could feel it in my coat pocket and it tormented me until I finally ate it. My empty stomach and deprived mind were satisfied for a while but, at night, my empty stomach would allow me no rest.

Mother said, "In the morning, I will divide the rest of the water. There will be less than a half a cup for each. Let us hope that soon we will get something to eat and drink."

After that, the people became quiet again. Pain and worry were deeply etched on their faces. We were ready to face whatever was coming our way but we were afraid and we were still hungry and needy.

During the third night, we heard another formation of bombers flying over our train. These planes seemed lower and sounded more powerful than before. We realized there might really be hope for us.

After the fourth night, early in the morning, the wheels of the train finally ground to a halt. We heard door after door slide open. Then we heard the loud and angry voices of the Nazis and the barking of their vicious dogs. Commanding! Demanding! Threatening!

When our door slid open, the first command to us was, "Throw out your dead." The dead lady's body was light; there was almost nothing to it. Two women picked her up, one at her feet and one at her shoulders, and threw her out on a snow drift. When the boy saw his mother being thrown out like a bag of trash, he buried his head on Mother's shoulder to muffle his sobs. We all ached for him and in our hearts we cried with him but we had no time and no means to help him mourn.

The destruction of life that we witnessed every day is difficult to comprehend. Our senses were paralyzed and we were incapable of thinking or caring, neither for ourselves nor for others. To survive, each of us had had to turn inward. We did not feel our hunger because we were numbed and our bodies were too weak from work. Our minds had shut down as a result of the abuse. We moved about like slow shadows with the fog of fear in our eyes.

I remember how one day, I began to understand that those who died were actually lucky. They did not fear or suffer any more. This lady was gone and no one could hurt her again but her young son would have to carry a double burden, missing his mother and coping with life on his own. Even at my young age, I was not afraid of death but I was afraid of being killed by my heartless enemy, starved to death, shot, gassed and finally burned in an incinerator like a bag of useless garbage. That scared me the most!

Mother told me later, "From that day on, your face became a lifeless mask as you did your work and lived with your pain."

We were ordered down from the boxcar to line up and be ready to march into the camp. The Nazis used their rifle butts, clubs and boots to strike men, women and children in order to get us to move and form into a column. We were weak, submissive and completely defenseless. We felt the harsh blows on our heads and backs but we did not even flinch anymore. We were dull and our will to live was almost gone. Nazis feared nothing and no one because they were strong and unbroken; we knew they were our brutal masters.

We finally formed our column to their satisfaction and we were told to march. As we marched past the other boxcars, we saw that most had thrown out more than one dead body and, in some cases, as many as five. As we approached the gates to the prison, we saw that machine guns were trained on us from the guard towers as we prepared to enter the concentration camp of Dachau.

A whisper was passed on through our column as we marched toward gates of Dachau, "Remember, try not to look too young or too old. Look strong! That way, you may live long enough to be liberated." Liberation was on our minds!

After we passed through the gate, a Nazi officer sorted us: Men to the left, women and children to the right and weak ones with small children to the trucks where soldiers stood ready to push them aboard and send them to their final destination.

16. Dachau

Inside the camp, I saw the walking dead wearing black and white striped uniforms with white arm bands displaying either a Yellow Star of David or a series of black numbers. Their emaciated faces reflected the hell they were enduring. We knew that soon we would be joining them in their agony.

There were people of all ages, races, nationalities and gender in the camp. They all suffered from hunger, stumbled from weakness and many finally dropped dead.

I never saw any sign of pity on the faces of the young Nazi soldiers for those who suffered at their hands. I thought to myself, how can that be? Did not their mothers raise them to love and care for others? Did not their mothers show them how to love their friends and neighbors? Were they not raised in the Catholic or the Lutheran faith where God's love was taught? Where did all that hate come from that I saw in their eyes, on their faces and in their mean-spirited actions towards others? Are we not their brothers and sisters? Who can answer these questions for me?

At Dachau, everything was eerily quiet. The Nazis approached us with soft words on their lips, icy-cold indifference in their eyes, clubs in their hands, and no pity in their hearts. This was meant to keep the new group from panicking and causing chaos.

As I stood in line, I wondered how many people had been on our train. The line behind me stretched out of sight. After we were sorted and counted again, we were asked, "What is your name, country of origin, (they called us Russians no matter where we were from) educational status and life occupation?"

I remember when Mother told them, "I was a cook at the Polish holding camp at Grajevo." She was hoping to get a job in the kitchen for herself and me. But there were many other jobs, work in the stone quarries, building and repairing roads, sweeping and picking up small stones and large rocks, doing laundry, and brutally hard work for men in the munitions plants that were located near the camp in the town of Dachau. In summertime, there would be a great demand for farm hands.

Someone said, "Not far from Eschenhof, inmates are cutting turf in the marshes. These inmates stay in farm buildings at night and eat real food because the old farmer is a kind and God-loving man."

The Nazis checked our mouths to harvest gold crowns or gold fillings; only the Jewish inmates had gold in their mouths. The Nazi officer smiled sweetly and assured them that it would not hurt. Then, their teeth were knocked out with the butt of a pistol and the bloody treasure was tossed carelessly into a box with the other gold teeth.

Our heads were shaved, men, women and children alike. Brokenhearted, I sobbed for the loss of my blond hair. I thought to myself, what else do they want from me? What else do I have to give up?"

A lady next to me put her arm around me and comforted me by saying, "Do not cry for your hair, my dear child. Cutting off your hair means that they plan for you to stay and work here; this means you might live long enough to be rescued."

Next, our heads and our shoulders as well as our blankets were sprinkled with white powder. Later, I learned it was used to kill head and body lice.

We were guided to another building where they took our old worn-out leather shoes and gave us a pair of Dutch-style shoes with wooden soles and canvas tops. We wore those shoes without socks and our feet turned blue and stiff from the freezing weather. Next, each inmate was given striped pants and a shirt. Later on, Mother and I traded our uniforms since hers was too small for her and mine was way too large for me. We all were surprised and felt lucky that they let us keep our blankets.

It took us a whole day to be processed into the camp. By the time it was almost dark, only one more procedure was still on the agenda. We were to be tattooed with the numbers on the inside of our lower left arm. Somehow, Mother was pushed ahead of me by the guards while I was kept behind with the other children.

By the time it was our turn to be tattooed, the Nazi Medical Officer was visibly tired, red-faced from drinking Schnapps, and fuming mad. He was shouting to one of his assistants for a new tattooing instrument and yanking kids to hold us back. We were scared, tired and all we wanted to do was slip past him. By the time it was my turn, he was furious again. He grabbed my arm and yanked me into a position to be tattooed but again the instrument would not work. He was directing angry words at me but still, the tool would not work. In a rage, the officer jerked me past his stand, called me a dirty dog, slammed the defective instrument on the table and walked off. I did not know what to do. His helpers, with great relief, just pushed me and six other children past the station.

We had to stand in another line for food but before it was our turn, they ran out of food. We went to our assigned barracks with nothing to eat for the third day; we had been without food for two days before we arrived at Dachau and the one full day in the camp. We were hungry but too tired to feel any hunger pangs because our bodies were too numb to react.

After walking forever, we finally found our barracks. Mother and I were too tired to care about the people who were still talking to each other all around us. Some of the people in our barracks were inmates who had been there for some time but most were new.

Mother reminded me that, "Soon, we need to talk." But I knew it was impossible to have a private conversation with so many people around us.

Learning about Camp Life

I remember how Mother and I listened to the others who were trying to warn us about the camp life, the rules and the punishments.

One lady who slept next to us said, "We all sleep dressed for warmth and to keep our things from disappearing during the night, especially our shoes and belts. These items are the most valuable possessions we have. With a belt you can repair your shoes, hold up your pants and keep your coat from flapping open in the cold wind when the buttons are all gone."

Another lady told us about the medical experiments that were conducted in Dachau. The Nazis claimed that these experiments were done for the good of humanity. She said, "The Medical Officers had access to the entire camp population, and thousands of young and strong inmates were selected for experiments. That is how I lost my sister. They took her and I never saw her again. Now the medical experiments are closed for good."

She added, emphatically, "Praise God for that!"

Others told us about the rules that if broken brought on the most severe punishment: Attempts to escape were halted by open gunfire, no questions asked. We were never to exchange with others the barracks that were assigned to us. Roll call and countdown were held every morning. We were told, "Do not be late if you know what is good for you!"

If the weather was wet or cold, we had to stand outside longer than usual. We were told that the Inmate Guards were sadists. They loved to see us suffer every chance they got. That proved to the Nazis guards that they were doing a good job.

The old inmates also told us about the new gas chambers. They talked so casually about the gas chambers that it scared us. Life meant nothing to them anymore because they saw death every day. They said that Barracks X, built in 1942, was a bigger plant with a gas chamber and four incinerator chambers. The gas chamber was camouflaged as a shower room, but it had not been used yet.

They said, "Now Dachau is self-sufficient. No need to ship dying inmates to other camps for extermination. They can do it all here."

Mother said with a smile on her face, "Lorissa was lucky today. She escaped being tattooed because the tool broke down by the end of the day. Lorissa and five other girls were pushed to the back during the course of the day and they did not get tattooed."

A wise old inmate said, "She is unlucky, not lucky! Those who were tattooed looked healthy and strong to the medical officers and, most likely, they will live longer. But those without numbers are fated to be exterminated soon."

The old inmates saw that the talk about gas chambers, tattooing and other rules were making us sick at heart so they changed the subject.

One man said, "Did we tell you about the American planes that fly over this camp quite often? Each time they fly over, they come down lower and lower, as if to tell us that they know we are here. This makes the Nazi guards and Nazi officers mad as hell! Sometimes they get so angry that their faces turn red from yelling and shaking their fists at the planes. At other times, they take out their firearms to shoot into the air. This is what gives us hope. We love to see the Nazis scared and worried."

They went on to say, "Many things have changed in the camp over the years. They have cleaned up and hauled away by truck-loads piles of dead bodies that were stacked up in some places shoulder high. They were also burning lists and documents in the incinerator by the armfuls. The burning was done only by the Nazis and we could see they were working at high speed as if they knew their time was running out."

What Happened to My Mother?

During the second or third week in January of 1945, Mother did not return from her assigned work one night. The women in our barracks gathered around me with pity on their faces trying to comfort me, patting and stroking me with their loving hands. I suspected they had a good idea of what had happened to Mother but no one was willing to tell me. All I knew was that my mother was lost somewhere in a sea of inmates. I could not tell the difference between men and women. They all were emaciated with shaven heads and they all wore the same kind of uniforms. I wondered how I could find my mother in this place.

After a while, everyone went to sleep; they were worn out and weak from a hard day's work. Soon the lights were turned out and I was alone in the dark with my anguished thoughts. I cried softly for a long time and sometime during the night, I finally fell asleep.

When I woke up next morning, Mother was asleep beside me. With joy and relief I jumped on her to give her a hug and a kiss.

With tears and a painful expression on her face, Mother said, "Do not touch me! I hurt all over my body and I am sick at my stomach this morning!"

I was so happy to have her back. I had a hundred questions to ask her. But she simply said, "Please, Lorissa, not now, leave me alone. I need to rest."

At dawn, after we were counted and the work orders were given out to us by the Inmate Guard, Mother and I were told to stay and clean up our barracks. All morning long, I worked hard to get everything done for me and for Mother while she slept. The next day, Mother was able to get up slowly and gingerly and try to get back to normal.

The Secret of Mother's Coat

I remember how after we arrived at Dachau, Mother and I usually were assigned to separate duties during the day but at night, after we got our cup of soup, we came together in our barracks for the night's rest. Unexpectedly, we found the chance we had been waiting for.

One day, our group's first work order for the day was to go to a building from where an acrid stench was emanating. It was so strong that our eyes watered and we almost vomited. The smell came from a pile of rotten potatoes, carrots, onions and cabbages. Each of us was given a small paring knife and we were told to trim all usable vegetables, place them in a bucket and carry the contents to a large wheelbarrow. We were assigned to work in pairs; one trimmed while the other dug in the slimy cold mess looking for anything worthwhile to trim.

Mother said to me, "This may be my only chance to tell you about my coat." We had to work fast and we had to be careful that no one would suspect that we were passing information to one another. In this camp, the Inmate Guards would turn in their own mother for a hunk of bread and a chance to live longer. These Inmate Guards were more dangerous to us than the Nazis. Even though they were our countrymen who spoke and understood our language, they had no pity for anyone.

There were no Nazi guards in the building because the smell was too strong. As I moved around my mother picking out the usable vegetables and putting them at her feet, she took the opportunity to talk.

In a low but distinct whisper, Mother began to tell her story.

"Long ago, while we were still living in Kiev, I decided it would be a good idea to hide our family photo in my coat in case we were taken away from Kiev just as we were. It is the photo of your father, you and me. It was taken the last summer before he was taken away from us by the KGB. I thought about it for a long time before I decided where I would hide it. It had to be a safe place.

"I decided that the best place would be on the back of my coat just below my shoulders. I wrapped the photo in a piece of soft cloth and then in a piece of soft leather to keep it firm and dry. I sewed it in by hand under the lining of the coat in such a way that it was invisible to a casual eye. This was the only place that would keep the photo safe and wrinkle free.

"I was always careful how I placed my coat when I took it off. The one thing I worried about the most was wetness. Since we were taken from Kiev, there have been many times when I have been wet to the bone while wearing my coat. I have no idea what condition the picture is in now but I know it is still there. I can always feel it when I put the coat on or take it off.

"I am worried that if something happens to me, the picture will be lost forever. If you survive, you should have the picture of me and your father. It is the only link we have left between us and our family. If I should die or be killed, be sure to take the coat if it is at all possible. But, please, do not put your own life in danger trying to save the coat." When Mother finished with her amazing tale, I was mute and dumbfounded. How could I have been with her all this time and never noticed that there was something hidden in the back of her coat? I wanted to know more about it but Mother said, "It would be wise to stop talking now and just work."

Then, almost as an afterthought, Mother said, "There is one more thing I must tell you. Your white cap is dark gray now but the red trim is still bright red. It could catch an eye of a young Nazi soldier. To be safe, it would be a good idea to turn the red edge inside so it will not be visible."

The Desperation of the Living

I remember how cold that winter was in Dachau. It was much colder than in the holding camp in Poland. Day and night, my feet were numb from cold without relief. I wished I had a pair of socks. That reminded me of how people stripped the dead bodies for their shoes and socks. I also remembered what Grandfather had said about the desperate needs of the living. Now I wished that I could find a dead body with socks on.

The skin on my legs and feet was blue from constant cold. By now, I was only skin and bones and the cold wind was really getting to me. I felt the strength slowly leaving my body. Just going to the privy was almost more than I could handle, let alone doing my assigned work. I had to concentrate on putting one foot in front of the other as I walked; I had become one of the walking dead.

In those days, my life was mostly defined by constant fear and gnawing hunger. I did not fear the consequences of childish pranks as a child growing up in a normal life would; I feared the Nazis and their punishment that could take my life. Fear was my constant companion. I feared everyone and trusted no one, except Mother.

On the other hand, Mother's life was defined by deep-seated hate and savage anger toward the Nazis. It had started while she was being brutally interrogated in that farmhouse outside the holding camp in Poland. From that day on and for the rest of her life, she hated Nazis with a hot passion.

The Shower House

By the end of February, the weather was sunny but still cold. One morning, as we stood being counted and waiting for our daily work orders, an Inmate Guard announced, "Your barracks was chosen to take a shower today."

I almost went limp from the thought of hot water running all over my cold, stiff body. I was thrilled with the idea and could hardly wait.

After we ate, the Inmate Guards marched us to the building where we were to take our long awaited hot shower. Inside the building we saw a huge gray room with numerous shower heads spaced evenly in the ceiling. We were told to take our clothes off and place them on the benches that were installed around the room. Everyone was reluctant to remove their clothing since the Inmate Guards were standing inside the room by the door watching us.

Soon, the guards began angrily yelling at us, "Take off your damn clothes and start taking the damn shower!"

Mother and I stayed close to each other as we undressed and we placed our things close to each other not far from the door. The women who were already undressed started to move cautiously toward the center of the room. But there was no water coming from the shower heads. Then we heard the pipes starting to make a strange high-pitched noise that was followed by hissing sounds. We were cold, nervous and scared. Then, we saw the guards quietly leaving the room.

All at once someone screamed from the back of the room in a high-pitched voice, "This is not a shower room! This is the gas chamber!"

For a moment, everyone stood still. Then, instantly, the panic was on. Women started to run towards the doors before they were closed behind the guards. I stood watching but Mother yelled to me,

"Grab your clothes and stay close behind me." We broke out of the shower room like an explosion of naked women.

Most women did not have the presence of mind to grab their clothes as they ran outside. Outside, they ran in circles but could not find anyplace to hide. This created mass confusion, clothed inmates mingled with the naked women; this gave the refugees from the gas house some cover and safety for a little while.

Meanwhile, outside, the Nazi soldiers and Inmate Guards were laughing so hard that tears ran down their cheeks. Quickly, Mother and I ran straight to our barracks and got dressed. Many other undressed women came running in later. They grabbed their blankets to cover their nakedness and to keep warm. Later, the Inmate Guards brought back all the clothes that had been left behind in the panic to reach our barracks.

We soon realized that the shower room was not a place to gas us but because of the very cold weather, most of the pipes were frozen and that is why no water came through them. Otherwise, the Nazis would have shot us as we ran for cover. At the time, Mother was correct about her assessment that this was not a gas chamber but a shower room; but as time went by, she became convinced that this really was meant to be a gas execution. She held this belief until the day she died in 1995.

The Professor

One of the inmates in the camp was ready to snap at any moment. He was called the Professor because he was known as an intelligent and wise man. In his youth, he had studied logic at the University of Kiev. But now, people said, "He is living on the edge of insanity because he cannot make any sense out of what is happening to his fellow Ukrainians in Dachau." They said, "He does not care about himself but his heart bleeds for his countrymen."

The Professor was kind and encouraging to all. Once, he stopped me and asked, "Where are you from? How old are you, my child?"

"I was born in Kiev, Ukraine, on March 15, 1934. I will be eleven years old soon but I do not know when the 15th of March will be," I answered.

He looked at me with his sad blue eyes and said, "Eleven years old and look what they have done to you! You look like an old woman. I can tell you were a pretty child."

His remarks threw me into a state of panic. I wanted to be ugly and repulsive so that the Nazi soldiers would never notice me.

But the Professor was saying that I could be pretty.

One sunny morning, while most of us were getting our work orders for the day, the Professor ran past us at a breakneck speed toward the barbed wire fence. Without even a moment's hesitation, he began to scale the fence. He climbed like a fly, screaming with pain from the self-inflicted barbed wire wounds.

Nearby, several Nazi soldiers stood calmly watching the poor man's agony. When the Professor was halfway up the fence, where everyone could plainly see him, the Nazis raised their machine guns to their shoulders and blasted him full of holes.

They left him hanging there on the fence for days, a lesson we could not forget. Eventually, his skin tore away from the barbs and his clothing shredded to ribbons as gravity pulled his body down to the ground.

One day, as we were marched past the Professor's body, I said my own farewell to this brave Ukrainian man. His ID number on his upper arm was exposed for all to see. I felt so sad that I had never learned his real name. Even in death, he was robbed of his true identity.

"Hang On, We Are Coming"

The best days in the camp, were the days when the powerful American planes flew over Dachau. Their sheer numbers shook the earth and their power gave us hope. We knew the Americans were winning the war by the way the Nazis stared with hate at the untouchable American planes directly overhead. They seemed to be telling us, "Hang on, we are coming!"

17. The Last Weeks at Dachau

As the days wore on, the unrest among the inmates at Dachau and the Inmate Guards who had sold their souls to the Nazis became even more visible.

Most inmates were trying desperately to cling to the last threads of their lives. We all knew that the end of Nazi reign was at hand but we also knew that some of us were too weak to make it to the end. These had stayed strong this far because they did not want to die at the hands of the Nazis. All these tired souls wanted was to close their eyes, lie down and die in peace. They longed to be in a place where there was no more cold, no more hunger, no more pain and no more fear. They were ready for the everlasting peace.

As the days melted into weeks and the weeks became months, we grew more and more discouraged even in the face of all the hopeful signs that soon we would be liberated. We heard all about staying strong and being brave but our minds and bodies were too weak to grasp the great significance of that. It had been such a long, hard journey and the wait ahead of us seemed unendurable. With each day, I saw growing signs of resignation in others and I felt the same feelings within myself. We were ready to give up, lie down and die; that seemed to be an easy way out.

The winter months of 1945 seemed colder than usual. We had no reserves left with which to fight the cold and the hunger at the same time. Our bodies were mostly bones covered with skin and the cold was our greatest enemy. At night, I could not sleep. It took me too long to warm up so I could get any rest. I do not remember much about those last weeks in Dachau; I was preoccupied with my own survival.

When spring of 1945 finally arrived, we were surprised to still be alive. For a while, the magic of spring gave us hope and strength and, at first, the field work that the women did was fairly light. As the days became warmer and the work load increased, the demand to work harder was pressed by the Nazis and almost at once that took its toll on us.

It was said by many that our food was somewhat better and we could get a second cup of soup most of the time. Still, no amount of soup could satisfy our ravaged bodies and restore our depleted minds but it did help a little.

A few days after the frightening shower episode, a large group of male inmates were lined up into the usual columns and marched out of the camp. No one knew where they were being taken but many said it was a "Death March." We knew that no one in their condition could go far on foot or last very long. They had been moved out before they had a chance to eat their usual morning cup of soup but it was said that all of the men had been given a chunk of bread to last them for several days on the road.

These men were on their last legs, just like the rest of us. The women in our barracks were concerned for them. One of the women said, "Let us pray for those poor souls who have suffered so much and will suffer even more. They face a tough test from which none will return. We do not know how long they have been in Dachau but let us pray to God that they will live to see a better day. They deserve that. We all deserve to live."

I did not know how to pray without Grandfather's help. It was easy to believe in God on a sunny summer day in Kiev, with Grandfather by my side assuring me that everything would be fine and that God listens to those who pray. Remembering that,

I prayed my first sincere prayer, believing that God would hear me and would answer my fervent request to save these wretched men.

After the escape from the "shower house," the fear of danger, the excitement and the cold air had totally drained my body of energy. Again, I was barely able to walk. Mother kept saying to me, "You must hang on. Don't give up. It will not be long before we are rescued."

I was glad to hear that but all I wanted to do was sleep. I could hardly keep my eyes open.

The Inmate Guards said to Mother, "Let the girl sleep." But the next morning I was told to get up and get ready for the roll call. I was shivering from cold. This time, the Inmate Guard said, "Snap out of it girl, you cannot be cold, it is April."

Everyone heard that. For the first time in over two years, we knew for certain what month it was; it was April!

The American planes were continuing to fly over our camp and the Nazis were getting more lenient with the inmates by assigning lighter work, just enough to keep us busy. Rumors and suspicions were flying everywhere.

Some of the people asked, "Have you noticed that the Nazi officers are gone and only the low-ranking guards and soldiers are now running the camp?" And they wondered, "When are the Americans going to set us free?"

One morning, as usual, we were counted and given our work orders. I was to go with a dozen women to work in a field. We all looked weak and sickly and by the old Nazi standards we would have been exterminated weeks ago. But here we were, barely able to walk, let alone work, receiving our work orders. Since we were to be outside the fence, we had two armed Nazi guards with us; one was a young new guard and the other was much older guard.

"We do not have to go very far, just to that field over there," the older guard told us.

The day was warm and sunny and I could hardly keep my eyes open. My legs felt so heavy and rubbery that I could barely move them. All I wanted to do was lie down and sleep. Some of the women tried to help me but I was unable to respond. Besides, all of us knew that Nazis usually shot those who were sick and those who were helping the sick, and each of us feared for her own self.

The young guard started to prod me with the butt of his rifle to make me move. I knew I was lagging behind but, as hard as I tried, I could not go any faster. I knew that in the past, the Nazi guard would have shot me right there and left me lying beside the road but I no longer seemed to care. All I could feel was the gravity pulling me down.

While the young guard went to ask his superior what to do with me, my knees buckled under me and I went down again. I closed my eyes and a great relief washed over me. I felt as if I was floating toward the warm sun.

I heard the young guard shouting at me again but before I could open by eyes, I felt a stabbing pain in my upper right thigh followed by a scraping on my thigh bone. At that moment, in my mind, I gave up because I was certain I was gone. My system was shutting down and I believed I was dying. Through barely opened eyes, I saw the young guard standing over me and holding his rifle with bayonet attached. A rush of adrenaline and a jolt of fear caused my whole being to come alive. I could see the guard looked angry. After the initial stab and bone scrape, I felt no more pain, nothing but numbness.

I must have passed out for a moment. Then I felt someone touching my upper thigh. In shock, I sat up; I had been taught from early childhood never to let anyone touch my thighs or my legs. I saw that the young guard was bandaging my thigh with his white handkerchief. I must have been his first victim and he had not yet become hardened by years of brutal service in Dachau. It was obvious to me that killing and inflicting pain on others were actions that were new to him. Regret was etched on his face.

He said to me, *"Bitte, auf stand."* (Please, stand up.) With the help of two other women who were not much better off than I, I managed to get up and, somehow, we all staggered back into camp.

The next morning when I woke up, I found a puddle of blood under my stabbed leg. Overnight, the guard's snow-white handkerchief had turned brownish-red with blood and dirt.

When Mother saw the puddle of blood, she said, "Where in the world did all this blood come from? You were nothing but skin and bones. Look at you. You are white as a ghost."

I did not care how I looked. I only knew that the room was swimming before my eyes, I felt hot and my mouth was dry. More than anything, I wanted a sip of water.

"Please, someone, give me a drink of cold water," I begged.

18. The Day We Had Lived For

The next time I opened my eyes, I was in a nice, clean room where doctors and nurses were working around me. The room was one that formerly had been occupied by officers when the Nazis still ruled Dachau with a sadistic iron fist. It was here that they dealt out death sentences with pitiless cruelty; a madness against humanity that was carried out in the name of their Glorious Fuehrer, Adolph Hitler.

As soon as I opened my eyes, I saw my mother and she was smiling. "My child," said Mother, "You have missed the most important day of your young life, the day of your liberation!"

Later, Mother told me, "For many days after we were liberated, you were gravely ill. Your leg was swollen double in size from infection. You lost a lot of blood and most of the time you looked lifeless. But after several days, the doctors said to me, 'Soon your daughter will be well enough to walk and play with other children.'"

When Mother told me that, I could not imagine running and playing like a child. For too long, I had been an adult dealing with serious issues of life and death. I did not know how to be a child. As I began to regain my health, the world seemed brighter and I felt happy for the first time in over three years.

But it was not so with many other inmates, mostly men. Because of their starved condition, these inmates had eaten too fast and too much. None of us could stop eating as long as there was food in front of us. As the result of this, many of the men developed bad cases of bloody diarrhea and profuse vomiting. In the end, most of these poor men died. It was so sad to see them go just when they had a chance for a new and better life. We learned that our bodies were too weak to assimilate rich food in large amounts.

The whole idea of being free was more than I could handle. I could not bring myself to remember how it used to be when I was just a little girl and there was no war, when I lived with my grandparents and there was love and joy in our home. I did not want to think about how an innocent child like me became a mature eleven-year-old with much hard-won wisdom and many painful memories. I did not know how I had survived the indescribable sufferings of the past three-and-a-half years of my life. I wondered if I would be able to forget the atrocities of the concentration camp and be able to lead a normal life.

Since I had missed most of the liberation day activities and the events of the days leading up to it, everyone was more than willing to fill me in on them. This is what I was told:

The last few days before liberation, in some ways, were strange and not at all the way we thought it would be. Each day, the Nazi staff in the camp noticeably diminished and the inmates were pretty much left to their own devices.

Many were agitated and fearful. Some said, "Before the Nazis abandon this camp, they will line us up and shoot us all like the dogs they always said we were."

Our excitement was impossible to contain. We knew that soon we would be free. Still, we had to be careful not to let the Nazis see what we knew.

There was a discussion about where we would hide if the Nazis were coming to kill us at the last moment. It was clear that there was no place in the camp where we could hide from the Nazis and their vicious bloodhounds. Once more, we felt that familiar hopeless feeling. Again, we were unable to help ourselves.

The Inmate Guards were scared and possibly regretted being so harsh in the past to their own fellow man. Now the time had come when they had to face us without the support of the Nazis. Most of the male inmates hated the Inmate Guards even more then they hated the Nazi guards. After months of brutal treatment at the hands of Inmate Guards, bloody revenge was on most of our minds and the Inmate Guards knew it.

At first glance, everything seemed normal in the camp on the 28th of April. We all went to bed early but sleep eluded us. We talked late into the night about many things but mostly we wondered when the Americans were coming to free us. When all the problems had been discussed and other subjects were exhausted, we turned our attention to food.

Someone would say, "You should taste my mother's Borshch, she could make the best Borshch in all Ukraine."

Then someone else would say, "That is nothing, you should taste my mother's pirozhki."

We would all close our eyes and salivate. This went on until one by one we all fell asleep.

On the morning of April 29th, the camp seemed unusually quiet. We did not hear the Nazis yelling or their dogs barking. One after another, we got up slowly and cautiously went outside to see what was going on in the camp. Some of the first inmates to go out came back breathless to report that the Nazi headquarters were empty with the doors flung wide open. Then, the next person came to tell us that the gates to the camp stood wide open also and that there were no soldiers in the watch towers to shoot us down.

It was also reported that the Inmate Guards were nowhere to be found. They had disappeared! But where did they go? One thing we knew for certain, the Nazis would not have taken the Inmate Guards with them because there was no love between the two groups. It was strictly a symbiotic relationship where each needed the other. Consequently, the Inmate Guards had no allies. The Nazis used them and discarded them and they were hated by those they had treated so harshly.

During our time at Dachau, most of us had been unwilling to betray our own countrymen for favors or even to save our own necks. But the Inmate Guards were not only willing to betray us, they were often more brutal to their own countrymen than the Nazis were.

There was great relief as well as surprise among the people to realize that we were still alive. We had truly believed we would be shot before the Nazis left the camp. Now, all of us stood looking around *and waiting for something to happen, but we did not know what to expect.*

We thought we were rescued but we did not feel free. Where are our liberators? That was our question. The Nazis are gone, so who is in charge? We wondered, "Should we stay in the camp and wait or should we go in search of our heroes."

We were confused in our minds and it was written on our faces. Then we heard heavy machinery rumbling in the distance. This roaring sound was followed by the sight of a huge cloud of dust in the road. In a few minutes, we saw the tanks and trucks coming.

"Look, look, the Americans are coming!" was our elated cry. Our joy was mixed with tears. It was indescribable. The idea that we had been rescued was too good to be true. But it was true!

Then, insanity broke out; we were laughing and dancing and hugging and kissing and yelling and crying. We were rejoicing and expressing our boundless gratitude to God and to the Americans. It was pure joy! It was like nothing we had felt before or will ever feel again. It was the unbelievable realization that our dreams had come true and our most fervent prayers had been answered. It was all of that and so much more. We were free. We had survived against all odds and now there was hope for us!

We were given food and drink until we were sat-isfied. Then the doors to the showers were opened for us to use. We were able to take showers without fear but we never forgot what had almost happened to us. A few days after liberation, we were moved to a safe place that did not remind us of Dachau but where we could still be together. We were given clean used clothes to wear—almost anything would have been better than what we had on our backs—decent underwear and good shoes.

All these things took place while I was still sick and unaware of what was happening. It was not un-til later that I learned what went on in the camp and in the hearts and minds of my fellow inmates.

April 29, 1945, is the date when all the inmates in Dachau were liberated by the American Forces.

Now, the Gates of Hell are open wide to those who want to see where we lived and where most of us died.

These open gates at Dachau are a symbol to the world that those who wish can enter, stay awhile, and leave at will. As inmates, we had no choice; when we were forced into the concentration camps, we were fated to stay there until we died. A few of us survived but we were only a handful compared to the numbers that perished.

262 I Remember . . .

19. In Search of Safety

I remember how, as soon as we regained our strength, other concerns loomed large on our horizon. Rumors spread rapidly all through our group. It was said that Germany would be divided into three sectors: American, English and Russian. Many people did not want to go back to live under Communism. They said, "We know what the west has to offer and we know that life would be better for us than it would be in communist Russia."

Later on, we learned that there were many more people who felt the same way as we did. We were afraid, now, that we would be trapped in the Russian sector with no choice as to where we wanted to live.

Everyone had his or her own idea of what was best for them but there were some people who really knew what they were talking about. One man in particular said, "We need to get out of Germany and wait somewhere else until all the sectors are established and known to all."

Mother said to me, "This makes sense."

But I was confused and concerned. All I wanted to do was go home to Kiev. I started to cry and beg Mother to go home.

"What will we go home to?" Mother asked. "Grandfather is gone and I am sure Grandmother was not able to survive the last three years without us. We have no reason to go home. There is nothing left there for us."

That was a new and painful revelation to me but, in time, I realized Mother was right.

In a short time, groups were formed and each group made the decisions that would be best for them. Our group was small with only eight people in it but we had a knowledgeable man to head and direct us. His name was Ivan; he was the only man in our group of seven women. Like our friend in Kiev, this Ivan, too, seemed to be a kind and compassionate soul.

We felt fortunate and much safer to have a man with us but we all had a say in every decision that was made along our journey. Ivan was able to acquire a map from an American soldier and he determined the best route to France. And so, one morning, we set out with map in hand and little of anything else and started walking toward France.

Part Four
The Long Journey Forward

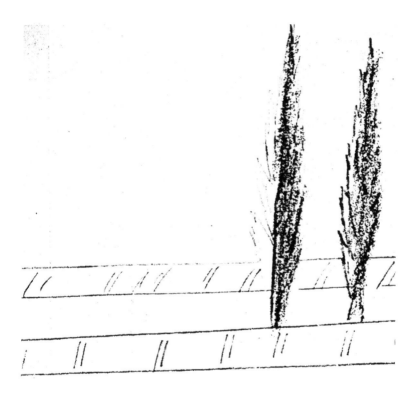

266   I Remember . . .

20. Setting Out

B efore we set out on our journey, we discussed
our great fear of the German people with whom
we would be coming in contact. Ivan put our fears
to rest.

He said, "Do not worry; Germans are afraid of
us, and rightfully so. They think that we will seek
revenge on them for what the Nazis did to us."

It was well known that German civilians had re-
quested the American forces to return all inmates
back to their country of origin. But the American
reply was short and to the point, "You brought them
here; now, you will have to put up with them for a
while until they find a home."

Our group did not walk fast since we were not
very strong but we kept up a good and steady pace.
Our plan was to stay most of the time on country
roads, close to rivers whenever possible. At night,
we rested in the wooded areas for safety's sake.

As we walked along the country roads, we were continually amazed at all the stuff the Germans had discarded as they ran to get away from the Allied Forces. We came across things like baby buggies, heavy coats and Nazi uniforms. We could not use most of the discarded things but we were amused to see the Nazi uniforms that once had been so frightening to us now littering the highways and byways so harmlessly.

Each of us had some food with us that lasted us for the first few days. Then we learned that the trucks with American soldiers always stopped and gave us food, especially when they found out that we were Displaced Persons (DPs). After we left the concentration camp, we no longer were called inmates but DPs.

The American soldiers were kind to us but especially to me since I was the youngest in our group. I always got an extra Hershey bar. I must admit, from the first time I tasted those wonderful bars, I developed an addiction to chocolate that has lasted me a lifetime. Sometimes, when the trucks were only half full, we were offered a ride. All along the road, the Americans were helpful and willing to tell us, if we asked, whether or not we were on the right track; they were a great help to us.

Once we came upon a burned-out farmhouse.

The house was a total loss and some of the animals were lying dead here and there. From all the signs, it appeared that the fire had occurred a day or two earlier. Some of the chickens were alive but spooky, running from bush to bush while searching for worms. As we were looking around for anything that might be useful, we found a vegetable cellar hidden by a pile of burnt debris. In the cellar were some sprouting potatoes and onions that were still edible and several quarts of canned peaches. What a treat that was. That night we had a feast; boiled chicken with potatoes and onions and peaches for dessert. The now empty glass jars with lids would come in handy to carry water as we continued on our way.

That evening, the campfire was especially comforting as we rested around it. After Ivan had recapped the day's travel progress and we had discussed the plans for the next day, we were ready for the night. Someone in the group said, "We used to be called inmates, now we are called Displaced Persons but, in truth, we are Gypsies or people without a country. What are we?"

This sparked a lively discussion about our homeless state. Finally Ivan said, "I do not want us to be called Gypsies; my parents had no use for them. Gypsies in our town were mistrusted and hated because they stole everything they could get their hands on. I hope we do not come to stealing and become known as Gypsies."

After those remarks, there was a silence. Then, a woman asked Mother, "Klaudia, we know you are pregnant but how far along are you?"

There was another silence but this time it was a long, suppressed silence. Then, Mother simply said, "Yes, as you can see, I am pregnant but I am not sure how far along. In Dachau, we never knew what month it was or even what day of the month it was. But I think I am four or five months along."

Again, there was a long silence and I said, "I did not know you were pregnant."

Mother said sternly, "I do not want to talk about it anymore!" And, that was that! When Mother did not want to talk about that we did not talk about it and I knew well enough to keep quiet.

I do not know how many days, weeks or months we had walked when one day, Ivan said, "Look over there, what do you see?"

We looked up and with one voice yelled, "Railroad tracks." Ivan said to us, "We must stay close to the tracks. We must not lose sight of the tracks. If there are tracks, then somewhere there is a train that will travel these tracks."

Ivan was right; one day, as we were walking, we

looked up and saw in the distance a village and, as we came closer, we saw a railroad station with a train ready to go.

The German people were surprised to see us. They said, "You appeared out of nowhere, where did you come from?" We just pointed in the direction we had come from because we really did not know the names of the places we had been. But all we wanted to know was, "Is this train going to France and is France far from here?"

They said, "Yes, the train is going to France and no, France is not very far."

We said, "We need to go to France."

At first, they said, "*Nein! Nein!*" and then, they remembered that there was no Nazi force to back them up. Almost at once and in unison they said, "*Jah!*" They wanted to be rid of us.

The Germans hustled to make room for us on the train. They emptied out one compartment for six people and found room in the next compartment for two more. Everyone in our group was eager to get in and get settled. When Mother and I looked around, we saw that we were the only ones still standing in the hallway. Soon, the two of us were seated in the next compartment with four Germans.

The German Lady

It was not long before the train was moving at a good clip. At first, most of the German people in our compartment stared at us in silence but one by one they dropped off into sleep. Mother and I and an elderly German lady with an ironic smile on her lips were the only ones still awake.

The lady said to me, "My dear, how old are you, where were you born and where are you going?"

This much I could understand so I answered, "I am eleven years old and I was born in Kiev, Ukraine. We are going to France."

Still curious she asked, "But where in France do you want to go?"

I said, "We just want to be in France."

She squirmed uncomfortably in her seat as she asked me, "Tell me, child, is it true that you people do not wash your feet and you do not take your shoes off when you go to bed?"

Her questions made me so angry. I looked at Mother and saw that she was watching me with pride and amusement. So, I took a deep breath, and answered her, "Why do you want to know that? Don't you know what to do with your feet and your shoes at night?"

The German lady did not like being bested by a Ukrainian child. Angrily, she got up with a jerk and left our compartment.

After the German lady was gone, Mother broke out laughing until she cried bitter tears. She said, "The Germans still hate us but they do not know why."

I could not go to sleep that night because I was still so angry. Then I realized I had the answer to some of my own questions that had been plaguing me since I saw such cruelty in Dachau at the hands of the young Nazi guards. This lady was a Nazi grandmother who had helped raise her cruel-hearted, blue-eyed sons and grandsons. And in turn, these sons and grandsons without showing any mercy or regret had made the inmates in Dachau suffer and die. Even though the war was over, this lady still hated us and considered us to be subhuman dogs and swine. I realized that she was too old to change and I felt sorry for her. The Nazi doctrine had a far-reaching affect on most German people. They still wanted to believe they were the members of a super race.

Arrival in Paris

I remember that even through my deep sleep, I felt the train moving on most of the night. In the morning, the train pulled into a grand railroad station. We were shocked when we saw that we had arrived in Paris. We had wanted only to be in the French countryside and not in the capital of France. Everything was so much grander here. People were well dressed and there were so many of them. They were darting in and out, every which way. I felt just like one small ant among thousands.

After we regrouped and pulled ourselves together, we walked out of the grand station in a daze but we held our heads high. The change was so abrupt and so overwhelming, it took our breath away. We wanted a bath and a change of clothing but that was like asking for a miracle. The next best thing would have been to hide somewhere but that, too, was out of the question; we had no idea where to hide.

We had thought our clothing was nice compared to the striped uniforms we wore in Dachau. But now, as we looked at each other with a critical eye, we saw that our clothes were rumpled, torn and dirty. We only had one set of clothing without a spare and we had come a long way in what we were wearing. I felt like a ragamuffin and I was too ashamed to be seen in the bright light.

We had no food and no means by which to buy any. The French language was totally unfamiliar to us and the people were in such a big hurry that no one seemed willing to stop and listen to us. When we tried to approach someone, we were pushed aside in a very rude manner.

We walked around in a daze, wondering what to do. It had been more than twelve hours since we had had anything to eat and we did not know where or when our next meal would be. We looked to Ivan for answers but all he could say was let us wait and collect our thoughts before we decide what to do. We walked until we found ourselves in a nice cool park where there were fountains and little creeks running here and there but there was no drinking water.

Ivan said to us, "Let us separate into groups of twos or threes and go in different parts of the park to see what we can find that would be helpful to us."

The park was huge and I was concerned that we would get lost. After several hours of laborious walking, we returned to our starting point. Some said they had found a thicket of bushes where we could sleep at night. Others had noticed people drinking out of a clear stream and they thought we could get a drink there. But other than that, there was nothing else that could be helpful.

We saw American soldiers in Paris but they did not pay any attention to us. Apparently, we did not stand out in a crowd as we had in the deserted German countryside. Ivan noticed an elderly man across the street and went to ask him for help. From a distance, we watched him and silently prayed that the man would help us.

The old man was no help to us but he did point us to another man who, by a stroke of luck, knew a little bit of Russian. He told us that we were not far from a place where war-torn people could go for help. Armed with this information and directions, with hope in our hearts, hungry and tired, we set out on another pilgrimage. Soon we came to a large building that had once been used as a warehouse. The building had been converted into a kitchen, an eating area and a resting area on the first floor; on the second floor, there were cots, hundreds of them, for people to sleep on. There were no blankets and no pillows but that was all right with us; it was late May and the weather was quite warm. We did not need pillows and blankets, only a safe place to sleep and to be close to those we knew and trusted.

The most exciting discovery, however, was to see the many people who were there. At a glance, we could see that we all were in the same boat. The others told us, "We are waiting for a train to take us back to our homeland."

We all in our group were facing the same plight but none of us was willing to give up our dream of finding a new home in a new country; America was on the top of the list for all of us.

There were many people there from Dachau. At first, we did not recognize each other. Our hair had grown longer, we had smiles on our faces and we had gained weight. We all looked like different people. It was no wonder we did not recognize each other. Some of the women were from the same barracks where we had slept practically next to each other for months. We were so glad to see each other and to know that so many of us had survived.

Lost in the Paris Subway

By talking to the other people at the shelter, we found out that the Soviet consulate was located somewhere in the middle of Paris. We were told that it was a very difficult place to find.

They said, "It is important to register with the Soviet Ambassador as soon as possible. The Soviets are paying for our food and our stay here. To get there, you must take the subway. Do not forget to change trains at the right station."

We were given a map with the name of the station circled in red and were told, "Do not forget, the French are the rudest people on earth. Do not ask them for help unless all else fails. And remember, you must be at the consulate before five o'clock or you will find the doors locked until next morning."

Ivan said, in an arrogant way, "It cannot be that difficult. I have been in the Moscow subway many times and it was easy."

But the people who gave us the instructions were right. After all the warnings, we were scared and nervous right from the beginning and, in our haste, we took the wrong train and became hopelessly lost. We spent the rest of the day trying to backtrack and unravel our mistakes.

At this point, Mother volunteered me by saying, "Lorissa can speak French and German. She is talented with languages. Let her help us."

I was shocked and embarrassed. I did not like to be pushed into the spotlight like that. When I protested, Ivan totally ignored me. He pushed the subway map into my hands, pointed me towards a well-dressed lady and said, "Go ask her for directions."

When I approached the lady, she refused to look at me, and when I asked her for help, she pushed me aside and hurried away. She did not even give me a glance. By the end of the day, we were still hopelessly lost and, according to the station clock, it was thirty minutes past five and we were too late.

Tired and hungry, we sat on a bench in the subway thinking and remembering that first park we had discovered and we wanted to go there. But Ivan said, "There are many parks in Paris and I know we will never find that same park tonight. But we will find another park and we will stay there."

The same lady who had spoken of us as Gypsies before said, "We cannot get away from being Gypsies no matter how hard we try."

At that, we all broke out laughing and crying.

Then someone said, "We have been through a lot worse than sleeping in a park. Come on, we will survive this, too."

We found a park, settled down deep in a thicket of bushes and rested in peace for the rest of the night.

The next morning, we cleaned up in a nearby fountain the best we could. Then, across the street, we spied a man from the warehouse who was one of the leaders there. Immediately, we ran to him and asked for his help.

By noon, our whole group was sitting in the Consulate office answering questions and filling out forms. We were disappointed and sick at heart that we had not been able to escape the Soviets' grip on us but we knew that there was no other way out of France if we did not get some help.

After the paper work was done, we were told to go back to the warehouse. We protested in one loud voice, "Without any help to get there, we will perish for sure."

Begrudgingly, we were provided with a guide and, in less than an hour, we were back at the warehouse.

Waiting for the Train

A few days before we made our visit to the Soviet Consulate, we had noticed the two sets of railroad tracks in front of the warehouse. Ivan said, "That explains everything, the train will come here to pick us up and take us home."

We had become resigned to our fate and were ready to go home but the wait for the train was much longer then we anticipated. While we waited, little by little, we explored Paris and began to enjoy its parks on our own.

Germany had surrendered and the war was declared over on May 8, 1945, and the madness in Paris began. In the days and weeks that followed, people of all ages celebrated with gusto the end of the war. During the day, there were parades and one day, we were asked to join in the celebration. We were surprised to be asked. We had thought that no one even knew we were there. After all, they had been doing a good job of ignoring us. Most of us did march in a parade and, in the end, we caught the fever of great joy and we celebrated along with the

French people.

Food and drinks showed up seemingly from no-where, big bonfires were started right in the middle of busy streets, and several Nazi and Hitler figures were burnt in effigy. The wild parties lasted until late into the night but our group had not yet regained enough strength to stay up that late.

Weary but happy, we returned to the warehouse, gathered the people we knew around us, and talked until morning. I was sleepy but before I dropped off, I listened to serious discussions about war, death and destruction. The former inmates wondered if war was worth the loss of so many lives and the destruction of historic property, things that could never be replaced. Some wondered, "How could the Nazis occupy our land and kill innocent women, children and old people?"

About then, I was gone to dreamland.

We stayed in the warehouse for several weeks before we were told that the train would come for us the next morning. In the evening, Mother and I gathered all our belongings and placed them in a burlap sack that we found in the warehouse. Early in the morning, we were fed and given a sack lunch. Before we knew it, we were being loaded on the Soviet-built train with a big red star on the side of each coach. Immediately, we discovered that the windows were stuck and there was no way to get fresh air. The bathrooms were filthy and, in some coaches, they were plugged up and running over. There were big, fat nervous flies buzzing around our heads.

Mother said, "What did you expect, this is a Communist-run train."

We sat in the hot train for several hours before it started to move. There was an officer and several soldiers in charge of us. They walked from coach to coach telling us we must obey all orders and cooperate for the good of all.

Mother said bitterly in a whisper, "It has been a long time since I heard that Communist line." She was not happy, I was not happy and, looking around us, I could see that nobody was happy!

After the orders were given, the officer said with an apologetic tone, "We have water but we must be frugal to make it last. In the evening and in the morning, the train will stop and everyone will get a cup of water. The food will be waiting for us down the line in the morning or at least by noon. I would advise you to save your paper bag lunch for tonight. That way you will not be as hungry in the morning."

The train was not setting any speed records but it was moving and the officer and his soldiers were gone for the rest of the day.

We traveled through French and then German countryside and at dusk, the train stopped. We all got our cup of water. Since it was hot inside the coaches, the water was welcome.

When we fell asleep that night, the train was moving. The next morning, however, when we woke up, the train was standing still. We looked through our dirty windows and saw no civilization, only tilled farmland and, on the far horizon, clumps of trees.

Mother said, "Where there are trees there is water." I was thinking it would be nice to cool off in a river but, to my dismay, we were not allowed to leave the train.

The soldiers, without their officer, came around to tell us that the train had broken down and no one knew how long we would be stopped.

Someone in the back, who could not be seen, yelled, "Where is your officer? Is he afraid to face us with the bad news?"

Some of us gasped; under the Communist regime, no one would dare talk like that to soldiers or to people in authority. But most of us had gone through too much to be afraid of these young soldiers. The soldiers who were not used to such backtalking had to bite their lips and go on.

That morning, we got our second cup of water

and we sat in the hot train for the rest of the day. The sun bore down on us and it was unbearable inside but still they would not let us out where it was a little cooler. In the evening, we got only a half-cup of water because they said, "We do not know how long we will be here."

On the second morning, we got another half-cup of water and a bit of good news. The officer reappeared and said, "I will let you out on the shady side of the train and then I want to talk to you."

We could not wait to hear what he had to say. Finally, we were out and seated on the ground.

The officer said, "The engine is broken down and the new part can only come from Russia where they made the train. They said that it will take only a day or two longer."

Everyone groaned and I thought Mother would faint. She looked sick to me and to the women who came around to help her in any way they could but there was really nothing they could do. We needed water and food for her and for everyone else.

On the third morning, we got less than half a cup of water. I tried to give my water to Mother but she would not take it. The day was hot and clear but we were still inside the coach. The soldiers who had given us our last-half cup of water said, "As soon as the shade starts to form on the shady side of the train, we will let you out. The food and water should be coming anytime."

But we did not believe him because he looked as if he did not believe it himself.

21. Unexpected Rescue

As we were waiting for the shade to appear, we heard the roar of approaching trucks. Everyone, except Mother, jumped up and ran to the door of the railroad car to see who was coming. The cry was loud and clear, "Americans are coming," over and over again.

Mother sat there with a hopeless look on her face as if there was no news that could possibly help. She had lost a lot of weight and all hope. I was worried.

The Americans came with soldiers, doctors and medical staff. They brought water in large aluminum barrels and food, the kind they had shared with us when we were on the road. They passed out those wonderful canned beans, boxes of crackers, canned meat, canned fruit, Hershey bars, and boxes of sandwiches made with real meat and real butter. There were even cigarettes for the men. We were saying, "This is a miracle!" and everyone was happy and smiling.

After the people were fed and had drunk all the water they wanted, the doctors and nurses began to check those who looked the sickest. When they came to Mother, the shock showed on their faces. It was obvious to the doctors that she was pregnant and that her physical condition was in a serious state of deterioration. The doctor ordered a shot for Mother and then they marked her forehead with a red mercurochrome dot.

Since I was hovering close by, the doctor asked her, "Is this your daughter?"

Mother nodded her head vigorously and the doctor marked my forehead with a red dot also.

When all the sick people had been checked, the doctors and nurses gathered us up and loaded us onto the trucks; there were approximately twenty-five of us. We traveled for about an hour before we came to a huge house that looked like a wealthy estate. The building was being used as a headquarters and medical center for that immediate area. Around the estate there were tents of all sizes. To one side of the house, there was a large field where many trucks and jeeps were parked, ready to go at any moment.

As soon as we arrived, we were taken into the big house where the sick were given a more thorough examination. After that, we were installed in one large tent. It was roomy and filled with cots, complete with blankets, pillows and sheets. I could not believe the luxury. We ate at the big house and the food was more than wonderful. Some food items were new to us but we loved everything. Maple syrup became my favorite new food. To this day, when I eat pancakes with maple syrup, I remember with fondness that wonderful American field hospital of long ago.

As the people were getting better, they wanted to help the Americans in any way they could. We were all so grateful to them and we loved them because they were our heroes. The officers and soldiers were kind and helpful to us the entire time we stayed there.

One young soldier named Peter told us that he could speak a little bit of Ukrainian; actually, he spoke Ukrainian quite well. Peter was a great help to us by telling us many things about America.

He said, "My mother, father and grandparents came to America a long time ago. My sister and I were born in America. My grandmother died when I was six years old and my grandfather missed her so much because he had no one to talk to in Ukrainian. My grandfather was too old to learn English and so, little by little, he taught me to speak Ukrainian. Through our Ukrainian language, we bonded and became more than Grandfather and Grandson. We became best friends."

Peter's job was to interpret between us and the Americans when there was a need.

Every day, we walked to the big house for our meals. We ate in the same dining hall where the officers, soldiers and wounded soldiers ate. Our Peter was always there to help us talk with other soldiers. We lived there for over three months and in that time we came to love Peter as one of us.

The Baby Arrives

One morning, during the first half of October, Mother said, "I think I will be having our baby today."

Since Mother never talked about her pregnancy or about the baby, I really did not know what to expect. When the contraction pains started, it was all a big surprise for me. But I learned fast and by midmorning, I was helping mother like a professional nurse, doing what I was told to do.

In the afternoon, the doctor told us that it was time for Mother to come to the big house. She had several contractions on the way but otherwise the walk went well. When we got to the big house, they took Mother into a special room and I was told to go and play outside.

Behind the big house there was a dense stand of rose bushes where a month earlier I had discovered that a wild mother cat had had four kittens there. It did not take me long to tame the cat and her kittens. At every meal, I saved up some scraps for the cats. To tame them, I made them eat out of my hands. In no time at all, they were running to meet me when they saw me coming. So when I was told to go and play, I headed straight for the rose bushes. By now, the kittens' eyes were open and it was so much fun to watch them run, jump and play.

But after an hour or so, my mind turned to Mother. I wanted to know what was going on with her in the big house. Just as I went in, I heard Mother screaming and that was enough for me. I went back to the bushes to play with those sweet little kitties. The next time I went into the big house, I decided to try to get closer to the room from where mother's cries were coming. But just as I was getting close, I ran into a nurse at the door who told me to go and play some more.

Soon it was time for dinner and, after the meal, I took some scraps to the cats but this time I gave them the food and went right back to the house. In the big room, some soldiers were playing cards and others were writing letters. I was too tired play so I found an empty sofa and settled into a cozy corner by surrounding myself with pillows.

When I felt someone trying to wake me, I could see it was dark outside; I could see the nurse smiling but I could not remember what was going on. She took me by my hand and led me to the previously forbidden room. Once inside, I saw Mother sitting up and holding a tiny baby in her arms. She was smiling at me.

On October 17, 1945, Mother said to me, "I am happy that we have a baby boy. I decided to name him Edward. We are lucky it's a boy; I never chose a girl's name. Do you think he is a cute baby?"

I did not know what to say; the baby was red in the face with white spots all over. He did not look cute to me. But I knew the right answer to this question. I smiled and said, "I never saw a newborn baby before but Edward looks cute to me."

Mother smiled at me and I felt a great relief. Luckily, this time, I had said the right thing and had avoided the wrath of my mother.

I remember our last days in the field hospital when Mother was well and the doctors were satisfied that Edward was strong enough to travel. We were being prepared to leave but we did not want to leave. Nobody wanted to leave. This was such a safe and wonderful place to be, no wonder we did not want to go. Many of our friends already had moved to a Displaced Persons camp not far from the field hospital. With the help of Peter, we were told all about the Displaced Persons (DP) camp where we would wait for a visa to a new home.

The day came when we had to move on. Peter said, "We want you to keep your bedding and we also want you to have this big bag of white kitchen towels to be used as diapers." In 1945, there were no disposable diapers and Mother was grateful to have these washable diapers; it was a very practical gift.

22. Life in the DP Camps

In the five years from 1945-1950, we lived in three different DP camps, in three different parts of Germany. I remember how each time, we waited eagerly for a visa and, each time, we did not get one. It was difficult to qualify for a visa if there was no man in the family. Couples and single people were chosen first but our family had two strikes against us. As a single woman, Mother could have had a visa a long time ago. Mother and I would have had the next best chance. But Mother, me and an infant was an almost impossible combination.

As the DP camps emptied out when people left for their new homes, the rest of us had to be consolidated and moved into another camp.

The first camp we lived in was built to house German military families. The two-story buildings were built of brick and were very nice. Each DP family lived in one room no matter how many members there were but most families were small.

This camp was a nice place to live. There were many young adults who organized soccer games. We would choose a favorite team and in the evenings we would go to watch them play. But when the visas started coming in, the young people left to go to their new country and that ended our evening fun.

The second camp was an ancient place where the barracks were built of wood. Through time, the wooden barracks turned a dull gray and looked worn out and tired. The old wooden walls were a perfect hiding place for bedbugs. I suffered more in that DP camp than in any other. Every night after the lights were turned off, the bedbugs came out and zeroed in on me. Even though I slept with Edward, he never had one bite on him in the morning but I was covered with red bites all over my body.

To protect myself, I had an idea. If I moved the bed away from the wall and placed the legs of the bed in cans of water, the bugs would not be able to climb on the bed. But I was wrong! Those crafty, stinky bugs outsmarted me. As soon as the lights were out, they crawled up the wall, then onto the ceiling until they were over my bed, then they dropped on me. Next morning, the results were the same; again, I was covered with red bug bites that later became infected and caused me great discomfort.

The last camp was nestled in the Alps, near the town of Berchtesgaden. It was one of the premier Nazi camps in Germany. No expense had been spared when this camp was built for SS officers. The long two-story barracks were built of brick and had expensive hardwood accessories. Each family had a room of their own with an improvised stove to cook on. Once a week, we stood in line to receive our weekly food supply.

While we lived in Berchtesgaden, a large shipment of used clothes arrived from America. Everyone was excited about the prospect of getting something newer and different to wear since the clothing we had was getting shabby and worn out. The camp was administered by a capable and popular member of the Displaced Persons who had been chosen by his fellow DPs. In choosing a leader, we had our first lesson in the democratic process. Voting taught us about fairness and the importance of choosing the right person for the job.

But humans will be humans no matter what and where they were and greed often won out over doing the right thing. To dispense the clothing, the elected leaders chose those who were close to them to help; they picked members of their family and friends of their relatives. By the time the clothing was sorted into categories, shoes in one pile, dresses in another pile, and coats in another pile, etc., to make it easier for people to pick out the things they needed, the best things were already taken by the helpers.

The people were called up alphabetically but by the time most of them got their turn, the clothes were badly picked over. And for the people whose last names were past the middle of the alphabet, there was hardly anything left. Since our last name was Nossowa, all we got to choose from was a pile of worn-out wool socks that was heaped in a corner of the room.

Mother was disappointed and I was crushed. I had a vision of a nice dress to wear but I knew I needed shoes even more than a dress. Instead, I stood looking at a bunch of useless socks.

Next to me stood an older woman, who encouraged me to take the socks. I walked out of that place with an armful of light-gray socks and the lady, whose name was Tanya, at my side. As we walked, Tanya told me that we could unravel the tops of the socks, wind the yarn into skeins and dye it a nice dark brown color.

But I said, "Where in the world will we find brown dye in the camp?"

Tanya was full of enthusiasm and even more information. She told me, "I work in the kitchen and I see them throw out lots of dark yellow onion skins. I will save them and boil them. Now, don't look at me like I am crazy. I will strain the skins out and save the dark brown water to dye the yarn. A long time ago, my mother did this to die our wool yarn. You will see that the yarn will be a pretty dark-brown color."

Tanya was right. Not only did she show me how to dye the yarn and roll it up into balls but she also taught me how to knit. With her help and with her knitting needles, I made myself a lovely brown turtleneck sweater and a pair of mittens for Edward. I saved those knitted things for the day when we would be traveling to America. I knew I would be proud to wear my new sweater as Edward would his mittens.

I wore that brown sweater long after I came to America but eventually it wore out. I wish now that I had kept it as a keepsake.

The town of Berchtesgaden and the area around our camp was breathtakingly beautiful; it looked as if it belonged in a fairy tale. The massive mountains stood tall and grand with snow covered peaks that stayed white all year long. The evergreen trees were lush and the rivers were crystal clear. The wild flowers grew profusely and the Bavarian homes along the road were picturesque. But it was hard to appreciate the beauty all around us while we were so worried about our future. By fall, many of the people in our camp were moving on to their new homes while we were still waiting for our visas.

In the early spring of 1950, the administration of the camp offered an English class to those of us who were still waiting. They told us that it might help with our visa applications if one of us in the family could speak English. I was thrilled when they told me I was the first person to sign up. Then they asked, "Will your mother sign up?"

I really did not know how to answer so I just said that one of us had to stay home with little Edward while the other will take the class. My answer was acceptable to them and my name was first on the list. The days went by slowly as I waited for my first day of class.

The Smell of Chalk

The snow was almost gone but, here and there, there were small patches of icy rings that cracked under my feet as I walked. Since my only pair of shoes were worn out and full of holes, I was stepping carefully to avoid the puddles of melted snow. All day long, my feet had been cold and wet but the freezing ground did not stop me. I was on an important mission that kept me walking. I was going to my first English language class.

I had not been in a classroom since 1941, when I was seven years old and now I was sixteen. I had attended grade school for a year and a half in Kiev, Ukraine, before the doors of the school were closed and my education was interrupted. World War II imposed itself on my young life and profoundly changed it forever.

Even before I was a teenager, I remember how I longed for school and learning. As far back as I can remember, school and books held a special fascination for me. I craved an education because something within me was crying out for a higher purpose. I longed to explore the mysteries of knowledge.

Because there were no schools in the DP camps, I taught myself how to read Russian so that I could read books. Then I began to teach myself the English alphabet and how to read English. When I spoke English, however, no one could understand me since I spoke with a European pronunciation. Above all, I wanted to be a student. I wanted to catch up with other students of my age and reclaim the education that had been taken away from me because of World War II.

For days, everyone in the camp who had signed up for the English lessons knew the date, the time and the room number of our class. I will never forget that number, Room 27. As I entered the administration building, formerly a Nazi military headquarters, I faced a long dimly-lit hall stretching before me. It was obvious that I was the first one there. No other students were in sight. Slowly, with a pounding heart, I made my way down the hall and found myself standing in front of a door with the number 27. I pushed the door open and saw nothing but darkness.

From the hall, I groped for a light switch on the inside wall and turned it on. As my blinking eyes were adjusting to the light, I stepped into the room. At that moment, my senses were overpowered by the once familiar smell of chalk.

Instantly, tears filled my eyes, making everything in the room blurry. I could not see where to step next. In this emotional state, my chest felt like it would burst and sobs rose up into my throat; I was choking and gasping for air. This overwhelming feeling brought me down to my knees. But, typical of a sensitive teenage girl, I did not want others who would be coming to the class to see me cry. Just in time, I gathered my strength and controlled my emotions.

Eventually, the class began and I was proudly seated among a classroom full of adult students. With a smile on my face, I knew that my dream was beginning to come true. To this day, I often think about that first heart-rending experience and when I remember that evening I realize how lucky I am today.

Waiting for Our Visa

I remember how by early summer, the camp at Berchtesgaden was emptying out fast but we were still there with no hope in sight. All single people were gone, all childless couples were gone, all families with grown children were gone, but families like ours with a mother, two children, and no father were still there and waiting.

One morning we were called to the administrative office. We knew that was a good sign and our excitement could hardly be contained. We were hurrying and our hands were shaking so much we had a hard time getting dressed. Finally, all three of us were standing in front of a camp officer.

He said, "The news is good; in fact, it is unbelievably good. You have received a notification from two countries, one from Australia and one from America."

Another office worker said, "Because we need to empty out the camp as fast possible, we decided that you must accept the first visa that comes through."

We agreed with their decision but deep down in our hearts we wanted the visa to be from America. Mother said, "We do not have a choice but to do as they say. But no one can stop us from praying to God and trusting that our request will be honored by Him."

The next days and weeks crept by at a snail's pace and during that time, we thought only about our visa.

Then, in the early part of October in 1950, there was a knock on our door and a man from the office said, "Your visa to America just came through."

That was a day we would never forget.

In November, we were getting ready to go. We had to be given many required shots and our health was checked for any communicable diseases such as tuberculosis. Then pages and pages of papers had to be filled out, checked, corrected and filled out again. It was a great relief when all that work was done.

Next, we were told to be at the warehouse first thing in the morning. There, we were to choose a nice outfit for each of us. Mother and I could have a dress, a coat and a pair of shoes. There were so many nice dresses but some were too small and others were too large. In the end, we found just the right dress for each of us and a nice outfit for five-year-old Edward. His sky-blue sweater went well with a pair of dark blue pants. My little brother looked so handsome and he was so proud of his new clothes.

Mother found a nice pair of comfortable shoes but I fell in love with a pair of black shoes with small heels and trimmed in red leather. They were what every teenage girl dreams of; alas, they were too small for me but I would not admit it even to myself, let alone to mother. I hoped that with prolonged use, the shoes would stretch and be at least bearable to wear. But no matter how long I wore them, they never stretched and I was never comfortable wearing them.

Mother and I decided not to wear our new things until we arrived in America. It was a great relief to me, since this postponed having to wear my painful shoes for a little longer.

By the first part of December in 1950, we were almost ready to leave. Each of us was presented with a large manila envelope containing our legal documents and our own passport. We packed most of our belongings into one medium-size suitcase. The rest of the things, we gave away to those who were still waiting for a visa.

Early in the morning of December 11, we were loaded onto an American Army truck that would take us to the Port of Bremerhaven. By mid-afternoon, we arrived at the Port and, for the first time, we caught a glimpse of our ship. We were told it was a retired battleship named *General R. M. Blatchford*. Many years later, I found out from its manifest that this ship carried 1,221 Displaced Persons plus the crew.

23. Voyage to America

On December 12, early in the morning, our ship sailed from Germany to America. The weather was sunny, the winds were quiet and at mid-afternoon we saw the Cliffs of Dover. I was so excited and from that moment on, I considered myself to be a world traveler.

At dusk, we were called to dinner and at about the same time, the winds came up and the ship started to roll back and forth with increasing intensity. As we entered the dining hall, we noticed that there were no chairs to sit on and the tables had a built-in lip all around the edges. We learned by experience that the table-lip was necessary to keep dinner plates from sliding off as the ship rolled back and forth along with our stomachs. To top it all off, that night's menu was boiled tongue with boiled potatoes and sauerkraut; we were not finicky but on a stormy night, that was a bit too much.

The next three days of travel were wonderful, the

winds were calm and the sun was shining. Almost everyone spent their days on the deck, talking and absorbing the warmth of the sun. Mother, Edward and I found a sheltered corner on the deck where we could relax and enjoy being together.

The Storm

On the fourth day at sea, the sun was still shining but the biting-cold wind was whipping up a gale-force storm. While the sun continued to shine, fierce waves tossed and rolled the ship.

For the next four days, everyone on the ship, except the crew, was seasick. We were told to eat. The crew reminded us, "Force yourself to eat, just anything you can swallow, and you will feel better." But that was easier said than done.

On the second day of the storm, the sailors brought us a large aluminum container of saltine crackers. When the vacuum seal was broken with a laud whooshing sound, the smell of the crackers made us turn green and we vomited. This unforgettable smell of crackers lingered in my nostrils and in my memory for a long time. After I came to America, it was years before I could bring myself to eat saltine crackers; now I enjoy them all the time.

After four days of rough seas, the storm began

to die down and almost everyone in the belly of the ship started to recover but Mother was still in bed and still not feeling well.

Some people were taking showers while others were getting ready for dinner. Edward was getting restless and pulling at me to go for a walk. It was a long storm for a five-year-old boy. Edward wanted to do something, anything that was physical, and Mother wanted us to leave her alone.

So, we went for a long walk. We went from level to level, looking around and mostly killing time. Before long, we were on the main deck. It was still sunny and the wind was blowing first fiercely, then gently, but mostly unpredictably. For a while, we stayed close to the doors but that did not satisfy Edward. He wanted to get a closer look over the rails. I must admit, I was curious also. I wanted to see how the ocean looked after a big storm.

We were hanging on to each other as we moved closer to the rail. Suddenly, a strong wind came up and the ship lunged sideways. We lost our footing and started to slide toward the rail. That scared us and ended our exploration for the day. Years later, when Edward was an adult, he mentioned that scary experience to me and we confessed to each other that we both had been really frightened.

The last three days at sea were pleasant and before long, we were approaching New York City. On the tenth day, it was announced through a loudspeaker that by dusk, we would be pulling into the harbor. At that time, we should be able to see the city lights and the light of the Statue of Liberty.

On our last evening on the ship, we ate our meal in a big hurry and quickly went up on the deck. We were crowding close to the rail, trying to see the light of the Statue of Liberty. No one knew what exactly to look for; there were so many lights and all of them looked alike.

Someone yelled, "Over there, I see it."

Someone else said, "I see the bright yellow light. See it?"

But no one was really sure about what we were seeing and whether or not it really was the Statue of Liberty's light.

On the morning of December 22, the ship was docked and we could only see the concrete walls of warehouses and the immigration building. All the Displaced Persons were told to get our bags and debark in alphabetical order. We were led to the processing room where we had our papers checked and our suitcases inspected. Then we received our train tickets and instructions about our destination.

After we had lunch, which turned out to be our last meal together as a group, with tears and smiles we said good-bye to each other. I could see fear and excitement written on each face as we hugged for the last time. We walked out onto a street platform where taxis were waiting to take us to the next stop in our journey to a new home.

The Train Ride West

I remember the taxi took us directly to the train station. When we boarded the train, we chose to sit in a corner of a railroad car where we would be invisible to all who passed us by. It was the evening of December 22, and the people who were getting on the train were in a festive mood. They were dressed in their finest and carrying gift packages in their arms. Even wearing our best clothing, we felt shabby. We could not understand English too well; it seemed to me that everyone spoke too fast. I had tried my English language skills on the ship and I soon realized that it was difficult for Americans to understand me since I spoke English with a European accent, so I kept quiet.

As soon as the train left the station, porters passed by us with carts full of food and drinks. Mother was impatient with me because I was too shy to speak up and order anything. There were too many people on the train who wanted service and I knew that I could not compete with them. So, the first night on the train, we slept tired and hungry.

My angry mother was constantly pushing me into new and strange situations that I dreaded. I could not cope with her demands, like the time she pushed me in the Paris subway to speak to the lady when I had very limited French-speaking abilities.

Next morning, Mother was after me again. She wanted me to stop the porter and buy some food for us. Money was no problem for us since we had been given enough money for food until we arrived at our destination, the far western state of Idaho. But my shyness was a big problem for me. I finally promised Mother that I would stop the porter the next time he went by us and ask him to help us.

When I saw the black porter coming toward us, my heart began to pound with fright. Before I could get my courage up to speak, the smiling porter was coming toward us. This black man was kind and patient. He listened carefully to me and gave me enough time to express myself fully.

I said to him, "We are hungry and we need to eat but I do not know what to order."

He seemed like a nice man who was genuinely concerned about our well-being. His soft brown eyes and friendly manner were comforting to me. Immediately, the porter began to show us the things he had on his cart. He talked about ham and beef sandwiches, about other kinds of sandwiches, about cakes and cookies. Then with pride, he said "We also sell 'hot dogs'."

That was enough information for me. With a shocked look on my face, I said to Mother, "We must be careful what we buy. They sell and eat dogs in America!"

I chose a ham sandwich for myself, Mother took a beef sandwich and Edward pointed to a sausage on a roll. As the porter served us he said, "Here is your ham sandwich, young lady; here is your beef sandwich, madam; and here is your hot dog, young man."

I swallowed hard and looked at Mother and Edward but they were happily eating their food and I realized that they had no idea what Edward had selected. To stay out of trouble, I decided to keep quiet; what they did not know could not hurt them.

The kind porter gave us all a free cookie, a candy bar for dessert, and a Coca Cola in a real Coca Cola bottle like those we had seen in American magazines. With his first Coca Cola in one hand and a hot dog in the other, Edward was smiling and I could tell he was in heaven.

For three days, I wore my beautiful shoes and suffered every moment. Whenever possible, I would slip them off but then it was an ordeal to get them back on. My poor feet ached and looked red. I wished I had chosen a more sensible pair of shoes but I never did admit my regret to Mother.

Idaho at Last

I will always remember the day we arrived in Idaho. It was Christmas Day of 1950. The train was right on schedule, 2:00 o'clock, Boise time. We all were nervous but I was scared since it would be up to me to translate between Mother and the people we were to meet at the station. In a letter from Emmett, Idaho, we had been told that Pastor James Havens and Mrs. Havens would meet us at the Boise Train Depot. We had no idea what they would look like, but they knew us the moment we stepped off the train. They were friendly people who lavished hugs and kisses on us in generous measure. We were astonished at the outpouring of kindness toward us.

Outside the depot, we got into the back seat of their elegant-looking car; I first, Mother next, followed by Edward. Pastor Havens got behind the wheel and his wife sat next to him. On the way to Emmett, we rode mostly in awkward silence since all conversation was difficult enough when talking face-to-face; it was even more difficult to talk from the front seat to the back seat.

Once in while, Pastor Havens pointed out several points of interest to us. I did not mind the silence; it gave me a chance to collect my thoughts and control my emotions that had been bottled up inside of me for too long on this extended journey. For days, I had been close to tears because of excitement and fear of the unknown.

It was a cloudy day and as I looked out the car window, I saw what seemed to be a desolate and barren land on both sides of road. The rolling hills and the flat lands close to the road were covered with dry grass, tumbleweeds, and sagebrush. I saw no trees and I thought, how could people live without trees? How could they build houses and furniture? Then, in alarm, it occurred to me, where are the houses and where are the people? Where are they taking us? Mother and Edward seemed relaxed but I was in panic.

We came to the old Freeze-Out Hill road that took us through a deep cut in the hill. Even though the day was overcast and it was almost dusk I could see a beautiful valley opening up before my eyes. It was such a surprise to see a big valley with trees and many homes. In the distance, I saw a thick band of trees that told me a river was running through the valley. Facing us stood Squaw Butte. The sight was magical and breathtaking all at the same time.

With tears in my eyes and a lump in my throat, I said to myself, "This is the place where I will live and where I will die."

Decades have passed and in the not-too-distant future this prophecy of a sixteen-year-old girl will come to fruition as, in my seventies, I search my memories and tell my story.

Pastor Havens guided the car over to the right side of the road, close to the old monument, and stopped at the lookout point. He asked us if we would like to get out of the car and take our first look at the Payette River Valley, the place where we would live. As I got out of the car and planted my feet, for the first time, on the Gem County soil, deep down in my soul, I knew that this was my home.

In that earlier letter from Emmett, we had been told that Mother and Edward would live in an apartment next to the Anna Frint's Nursing Home where Mother would be working; I, too, was to live and work in a nursing home in Emmett. Pastor Havens said, "We will drop off your mother and Edward first and then we will take you to your new home.

I remember so well that first evening at Elizabeth Scott's nursing home. By the time we arrived, it was dark but the lights from inside were bright and welcoming. Pastor Havens knocked on the door and it was opened almost immediately. In the doorway stood a middle-aged lady, with a friendly smile and kind eyes. Miss Scott wore a soft pastel dress with a clean starched apron giving her a homey look.

Pastor Havens said, "Hello, we are a bit late but here we are." Pointing to me he said, "And this is your long-awaited helper, Lorissa."

Elizabeth opened her arms and drew me to herself.

All of this was too much for me. Again, I was fighting to keep my tears in check. Luckily, Pastor Havens and Mrs. Havens did not stay long.

As soon as they were gone, Miss Scott said, "First of all, I want you to call me Elizabeth."

I nodded my head in agreement. I did not dare speak since my tears were reaching the point of spilling over.

Elizabeth asked me, "Are you hungry?"

Again, I just nodded my head but did not speak.

We went into a clean, inviting kitchen where in the middle of the room stood the most beautiful cat I have ever seen.

Elizabeth asked me, "Do you like cats?"

Again, I nodded my head as my tears started trickling down. "His name is Blue Boy and he likes people," said Elizabeth. I knelt before the cat to hide my tears. At this point, I realized that I had no handkerchief. In desperation to hide my tears, I started to wipe my eyes and my nose with the sleeve of my coat.

Elizabeth gently took me by my arms, pulled me up and said, "Do not worry, everything will be just fine in the morning."

Then she picked up Blue Boy and placed him in my arms. He was purring loudly, like a well-oiled motor.

Elizabeth said to me in a gentle voice, "See, Blue Boy likes you and I like you."

I looked at her with a grin and we both started to laugh until we cried. Two hankies appeared seemingly out of nowhere, one for me and one for her.

"Do you know what I think?" she asked. "I think you are hungry and after you eat, you will feel much better."

Then, like magic, the round kitchen table was covered with a cake and a pie and a platter of meat and rolls and butter and milk. All these things were almost unfamiliar to me; I had not seen good food like that since before the Nazis occupied Kiev. We both ate and smiled and talked and I ate some more and we fed Blue Boy until all three of us were stuffed.

Then Elizabeth brought out the sweetest pink nightgown I had ever seen. "I hope it fits you. If it does, then it is yours to keep," she said.

I had not slept in a nightgown since I lived in the Polish village of Grajevo. I was overwhelmed by Elizabeth's kindness. Then she showed to me a small cute bedroom with a pink spread and a pink pillow trimmed in white lace on the bed.

"This will be your bedroom, I hope you like it," she said.

I could not believe all this was just for me. I was overwhelmed again.

Elizabeth asked me, "Would you like to take a bath and then go to bed?"

I kept saying, "Yes" and "Please" and "Thank you." I did not know how to handle all this kindness. To top it all off, Elizabeth had special towels hanging in the bathroom just for me. I had not expected all this and I was crying tears of gratitude again. I was a mess of emotions but I hoped that by morning, things would seem more normal and I would be more comfortable.

In the morning, as soon as I opened my I eyes, I parted the curtains to see what was outside the house. First, I saw a busy street running past the house. There were several small business buildings but one building just across the street caught my eye; it had the words 'Purina's Feed and Seed' printed on it. I wondered what that might mean.

But I had no time to dwell on this question at the moment; instead, I quickly got dressed. I was worried that I might have overslept and Elizabeth might be angry with me.

When I walked into the kitchen, Elizabeth was surprised to see me up so early. She said, "See, we are so much alike; I, too, am an early riser." We laughed and then she offered me breakfast.

At the table, I said to Elizabeth, "What does it mean 'Poorinas Fad and Sad'?"

She looked at me mystified and asked, "Where did you see that?"

When I told her, she laughed again and said, "In English, it is said 'Purina's Feed and Seed.'"

"But what does that mean?" I asked again.

Elizabeth said, "The store across the street sells to farmers, Purina foods for animals to eat and Purina seeds to plant in the field."

I felt stupid for asking such a simple question and my face turned red.

"Do not worry, that is how you will learn," Elizabeth said in a kind voice. Then she said, "You already know many English words and I will help you to pronounce them correctly."

As the days went by and I heard English all around me, I quickly started picking up correct pronunciations.

In the mornings, I helped serve breakfast to five elderly ladies who lived in our small private nursing home while Elizabeth dispensed medications and their clean clothing for the day. I also helped with bathing, dressing and combing their hair. The ladies spent most of their days sitting in the living room, waiting for their families to come and visit them but, sad to say, they almost never came. It did not take them long to adjust to my foreign accent and, before I knew it, I found that they liked me.

They said, "It is so nice to have a young person living with us." Some said I reminded them of their granddaughters or their daughters.

When the morning work was done, and after Elizabeth and I had washed dishes in the kitchen, we did hand work, like ironing, mending and preparing vegetables for dinner. While working in the kitchen, Elizabeth liked to listen to her favorite 'soap operas' on the radio. These turned out to be my main source of learning English grammar and pronunciation. As I listened to these high-drama programs, I picked up dozens of new words each day. With Elizabeth at my side, I had an instant translation just for the asking. Before long, I was able to communicate with ease and be understood.

From the beginning, Elizabeth and I worked well together and, as we worked, we got to know each other better and better. She was a bright lady who could tell factual stories in a most interesting and detailed way. I began to learn about Idaho, about America, about Elizabeth's family and her childhood. She told me that she had never married because her sweetheart was killed in World War I Years later, Elizabeth showed me a ragged bundle of love letters from him that she kept tied up with pink ribbon.

Once, I asked her, "Why didn't you marry someone else?"

She simply replied, "I never found anyone I could love as much as I loved Bill."

Elizabeth told me all about her mother, Anna Leeper Scott (1867-1944), who had died six and a half years before I arrived in Emmett. Elizabeth said, "I missed my mother so much." Then she told me that she had been praying to God to send her someone she could love. Elizabeth firmly believed that God answered her prayers by sending me to be her special companion. I was also grateful to God that He had paired me up with Elizabeth. Only God could have matched us up so well.

Elizabeth was a devout Christian who never pushed her beliefs on others. Her whole life was a testament to her God and her church. She attended the First Baptist Church in Emmett where she was the Sunday School Superintendent for many years. Every evening, she read her *Bible* and prepared the lessons that she would teach the following Sunday.

Mother and Edward seemed to be doing well in the other nursing home. Mother called me often and complained about things I could do nothing about. For one thing, she did not like living in such a small town, which she called "the village." For another thing, she expected me to hand over all my earnings at the end of each month. Finally, she was angry with me when she found out that I was thinking about going back to school. Mother was especially angry with me when I told her that I needed my earnings to buy new and better clothes for school so I would fit in and look like the rest of the students.

When Mother fulfilled her contract with Anna Frint during the second summer, she and Ed moved to Boise. After the first grade in Emmett school, Edward became known as Ed and he liked his new name. Mother continued to work in nursing homes in Boise and, eventually, she met a man who became her second husband. Hubert adopted Ed to be his son and gave Ed his American name.

Mother and Hubert's marriage was not a very happy one but Ed thrived in the Boise schools, in both his academic and his social life.

By mid-January of 1952, Elizabeth had determined that I should continue my education. She said, "You are too smart to waste your mind."

But I was afraid that everyone would find out how stupid I really was. Long ago, Mother had convinced me that I was worthless. I believed her. And why not? She was the one who had given me birth and she should know. Mother had continually called me stupid, ugly, and lazy; eventually, I became the child she said I was, timid, withdrawn, and with no confidence in myself. That is why I was so reluctant to go to school and expose my ignorance to the rest of the community.

But Elizabeth would not let up. She kept up the pressure on me because she understood that I truly wanted education more than life itself.

One day, in desperation, I said to her, "O.K., look at me. I am a teenager and not a little child. I cannot go to school with little kids. They will make fun of me. They all have more knowledge than I do and soon they would find out how stupid I really am."

But Elizabeth had an answer for everything. When I finally had confessed to her all my fears and worries, with a gentle smile she assured me that everything would be fine.

After I took a test, it was determined that I was at fourth-grade level of book knowledge. Tutoring was arranged for me with Miss Daisy Chandler, a retired school teacher. From the second week in January until the third week of August, rain or shine, five days a week, I walked across Emmett for my three hours of instructions. I was instructed in English grammar, math and American history.

In the fall of 1952, with pride and fear in my heart, I entered the eighth grade. I went to school during the day and helped Elizabeth in the afternoons and evenings. Then, after dinner, I studied late into the night only to repeat my routine all over again the next day. But I was happy because my longtime dream of getting an education was coming true.

It Took a Valley

It took a valley of Emmett people to get me going. Many kind people helped me, partly because they liked me and partly because they wanted to help Elizabeth in her efforts to help me.

As I lived with Elizabeth Scott, I became a young woman full of hope, enthusiasm and faith in God. Each day I looked forward to a new and better day for me in America.

Many church people gave me nice things to wear; others gave me material to make school clothes and Elizabeth taught me how to use her old sewing machine. Dr. Whitsell, a local dentist, offered to do dental work on my teeth pro bono. I was too young to have seen a dentist before the war and after the occupation I had no chance at all. Even though he found many cavities, Dr. Whitsell kept his word and restored my teeth to a like-new condition.

Marjory and Ralph Haynes were good friends and close neighbors of Elizabeth. Their two young daughters became my first American friends. Dorothy Haynes was out of high school and working at the local telephone company when I began school but, through the years, we attended the same church and I had her daughter in my 4H Horse Club. We have always been good friends.

Donna Haynes was a junior at Emmett High School while I was an eighth-grader in the same school building. Every morning, Donna came by Elizabeth's house and for two years we walked to school together. It was extremely comforting to have a friend like Donna. On the way to school, sometimes we talked and sometimes we argued but always I appreciated Donna's company and advice. She was my first American friend who cared about me and helped me to understand the ins and outs of American school life.

The Baptist Youth Group took me under their wing and showed me the ropes. In the spring of

1951, they took me on a snipe hunt. I asked Elizabeth to tell me all about it, but she looked mysterious and only would say things like: "You will like the hunt. Most American teenagers have to do this. It is like the rite of passage for them. I promise, you will always remember the snipe hunt."

I was given an empty burlap sack and I was told to hold it open facing toward the south while my friends were going to drive the snipe into my bag; I had to catch at least one snipe to be successful. It was dark when they left me in the middle of a sage-brush patch holding the bag. Memories of the concentration camp flashed before my eyes. Then I heard a roar, and a big truck came speeding by.

That was enough for me. What I saw was a truck full of Nazis. I dropped the bag and started to run like a wild child. Every time a car went by, I hid in the sagebrush. The cars kept coming and going but I stayed hidden. Finally, my friends frantically started to call my name. I recognized their voices and I knew I was safe. I stepped out into the road for them to see me.

As it turned out, they were more scared than I was. They felt responsible for my safety and when they thought they had lost me, they were really scared.

From the time I arrived in Idaho, I faced many new and different challenges. English language was one and fitting into high school society was another. But the one thing I could not get used to or understand was the constant laughter and giggling engaged in by my schoolmates. I thought to myself, why are they so happy? Life for me was always serious and so often a matter of survival. I had no experience with light-hearted joviality. I was three years older than most of my classmates and my difficult life during the war years made me a very serious teenager.

The Emmett High School (EHS) kids liked and respected me but for the first two years, I was not a part of their inner circle. My new life in EHS was fulfilling but sometimes scary. My classes were difficult because of my English-speaking limitations and, therefore, my studies came before sports or anything else. I was a stranger in this community and when I found myself in a difficult situation, I often comforted myself by saying, "If I could survive the Holocaust, I can endure most anything that comes my way."

Once I was asked to join a tennis team by one of my classmates but I had never played tennis or any other ball game. Sadly, I realized once again that World War II had truly robbed me of my childhood.

In the beginning of my junior year, I was invited to a slumber party and quickly I accepted. Then I hurried home to ask Elizabeth, "What is a slumber party? Was it okay that I accepted the invitation from one of my classmates"

Elizabeth took a look at my puzzled face and laughed. Then she explained to me in detail all about  what a 'slumber party' was. I was surprised at the explanation and said, "But I never heard of such a thing."

And then Elizabeth said, "Those girls are from good families and it would be all right for you to go."

The slumber party turned out to be a rite of passage for me into the inner circle of high school society. That night, we engaged in many crazy-childish pranks. To my surprise, I found myself laughing and enjoying the slumber party more than I had thought I would.

The other girls said to me with wide-eyed surprise, "You are laughing and having lots of fun with us."

From that night on, my outlook on life slowly began to change and I felt that my classmates accepted me.

As I continued to attend EHS, I kept intently observing students, teachers and the people of Emmett. I came to the conclusion that I wanted to be assimilated into this wonderful community more than anything else in the world. But, still, in many ways, I felt different from everyone in the valley. I had a heavy burden of memories and experiences that held me back and kept me from being the happy and lighthearted teenager that my classmates and other people around me seemed to be. I could not shake the black cloud of my past that hung over me and stalked me day and night.

One evening, when I should have been studying, I had a most unusual visual experience, one that I will never forget. I saw myself unfolding a large, red western handkerchief and laying it out on my study desk. On this hankie I mentally placed my pain, my losses and all my tragic memories. I tied the corners of the hankie tightly together.

Then, in my mind, I dug a deep hole and placed

the heavy hankie into the hole and buried it. Standing at the grave of my memories, I promised myself never to dig it up and never to look at it or think about again. For over fifty years I kept that promise to myself and never looked back.

It was only when I decided to write this book that I allowed my buried memories to surface. As I examined each event again and as I wrote my memoir, I relived the unthinkable things that happened to me, to my family and to the people I knew.

During World War II, when the Nazis invaded Kiev, they forced thousands of Jewish and Ukrainian people into concentration camps where a majority of them perished. Those of us who survived the terrible ordeal of war were scarred for life. During those horrible years, everyone in the camps hated the Nazis with a burning hate that nothing would quench short of killing them. At first, I felt the same way but later on, I overcame the smoldering hate that I held in my heart just for the Nazis.

I believe that hate is like a lizard eating its own tail. That is how it was with Mother—she had been so scarred by her experiences during the war that she found it impossible to forgive. And so, bit-by-bit, hate grew in her heart until it destroyed every relationship and everything in her life. Long before she died, hate had consumed my poor mother until there was nothing left of her former self but her old worn-out body. She died in 1995 at the age of 84.

I know from experience that no one can be forced to forgive a terrible grievance but for me, forgiveness was the right choice to make. Forgiveness tends to benefit the forgiver more than the forgiven. I could not change my past but forgiving the Nazis was a gift of relief I gave to myself. I did not have any opportunity to reconcile with my enemy. When the Nazis lost the war, the officers and guards at the camp ran in the night like the cowards they were rather than face those of us who had survived their unbelievable brutality.

It wasn't until I came to America that I decided to let go of my painful past, to forgive and to move on. This action set me free to live a life of peace and happiness and to be a productive member of my community by helping others.

Today, I do not dwell on my memories of those terrible times in my past because I do not want to empower my enemy. I see myself as a survivor and not as a victim. But any identity label serves us only for a while. Eventually, we must let go of who we were and strive to become the person we want to be, a better and stronger self, one who appreciates the joys of the present and who looks forward to the opportunities of the future.

Epilogue

When I arrived in Idaho in 1950, I had lived through perilous and trying times and I had survived. When I saw what a wonderful and peaceful community Emmett was, I longed to become a part of the life of Gem County. I wanted to contribute and to show my gratitude for the opportunity to start a new life in the place that has been my home now for almost 60 years. I was especially grateful to the First Baptist Church and its members for sponsoring our family to come to America.

On July 8th, 1955, I married a wonderful man, John Wilfong. Together, we had a happy life and three wonderful children. All three of our children graduated from schools of higher learning, married and had families:

Basil John Wilfong married Cindy Von Strah and she had a daughter, Holly Bosworth Koechner, and a son, Tony Bosworth;

Greg Wilfong married Connie Spencer and they had a daughter, Jamie Wilfong Spangle, and a son,

John Wilfong;

Carissa Wilfong married Mark Summers and they had a son, Tyson Summers, and a daughter, Whitney Summers.

My brother, Ed joined the Army R.O.T.C. during his high school years and was awarded a scholarship to the University of Idaho where he earned a degree in Political Science. While Ed was a student at U of I, he met a lovely girl named Cathie and they married and had two sons, E. J. and Doug. Ed had a successful career in business and became a top executive for Continental Tire of North America, Inc. Ed and Cathie have three grandchildren.

After I came to America, during my school years and my early married life, I often had nightmares and "flashbacks", frightening images of those terrible days during World War II, vivid reminders of the pain and suffering I experienced in the camps not only from sickness but also from my never-ending fear of dying.

One rainy December morning, I was baking Christmas cookies in our kitchen and my husband, John, was feeding a large herd of cattle in the corral not far from our house. An important telephone call came for him. Quickly, I put on my rubber boots and my heavy coat and sloshed my way through the mud and sleet to deliver the message. (These were the pre-cell-phone days.)

At the corral, I saw something that caused me to have an *instant flashback.*

All the cattle in the corral, except for one, were busy eating at a long cement trough. A yearling steer stood apart from the group on a small mound of dry dirt. His head drooped, his eyes were closed, and his humped-up wet shape told me the whole story. He was sick! This was a picture of misery.

I was so clearly reminded of how I had felt when I was suffering from my eye infection in the *Straflager* in Poland. Like this young steer, I had had no shelter from the harsh elements. In the steer's case, it was the drenching sleet that was causing him pain and discomfort; in my case, it had been the piercing light of the sun that had shot bolts of pain through my eye.

I thought to myself that this young steer probably was doomed to an early death as I had felt myself doomed so many years ago. Instead, I had immigrated to America, a land where all things are possible for those who are willing to work for them.

In April of 1982, after twenty-seven and a half years of marriage, my husband, John, died of cancer and I became a widow.

During the next sixteen years, I worked towards the fulfillment of my ongoing dreams of getting an education. I had graduated from Emmett High School in 1956 and, after John died, I enrolled at Boise State University and earned a Bachelor of Arts degree.

One of the greatest accomplishments in my life was my graduation day in May, 1993, when I walked proudly down the aisle of the Boise State University Pavilion which was filled to capacity. My grown children and close friends were there to cheer me on.

Unexpectedly, as had been the case many times in the past, I was seized by an overwhelming emotion. This time, it was a feeling of great happiness and not of abject despair. My tears were tears of joy that accompanied the sense of pride I felt in my achievements. And this time, I did not care if anyone saw me crying.

My quest for education has never ended. Through the years, I have continued to take classes that furthered my education. Once Michelangelo prayed, "Lord, let me always desire more than I think I can do." There is a part of me that will not be content until I become all that I am capable of being.

In June of 1994, at the age of 60, I became a Peace Corps Volunteer. I served for two years in Hungary, teaching English as a foreign language.

Shortly after my return to America, I met Burt

Holt and, on August 30, 1997, this dear man and I were married.

When, from the top of the Old Freeze-Out Hill, I first saw Squaw Butte standing guard over the Emmett Valley, I was only sixteen but I said to myself, "This is the place where I will live and die."

I am now in my seventies; I expect that in time, my prophecy will be fulfilled and I have no regrets.

Time Line

June 3, 1910—Mother was born; she died in June 1995.

March 15, 1934—I was born.

September 19, 1941—Nazis occupied Kiev.

January 1, 1942—Grandfather turned 67. Grandfather was born Jan. 1, 1884, and died on Jan. 11, 1942).

Late February 1942—We were forced into cattle cars and shipped to the holding camp near Grajevo, Poland, where we spent many months.

Early March, 1942, Mother was abducted by the Nazis.

March 15, 1942, I was 8 years old.

Mid-April—I was kidnapped by Paul. Six weeks later, Maria killed herself.

Late May, 1942—I lived with Helena and Lazlo through 1943.

March 15, 1943, I was 9 years old.

Mid-January, 1944—I was returned to the holding camp and reunited with Mother.

March 15, 1944—I was 10 years old.

December, 1944—We were taken to Dachau. We lived there through April, 1945.

March 15, 1945—I was 11 years old.

April 29, 1945—We were liberated from Dachau by the U.S. 7th Army.

Late May, 1945—We were in Paris, where we celebrated the return of French soldiers from the war.

1945–1950—We lived as displaced persons in several DP camps in Germany.

October 17, 1945—Edward was born.

Dec. 12–22, 1950—We sail from Germany and arrive in America.

Christmas Day, 1950—We are welcomed to Idaho.

Did you borrow this book?
Want a copy of your own?
Need a great gift for a friend or loved one?

Yes, I want to have a personal copy of this book. Send me ____ copies of I Remember. . . & ____copies of A Gift of Life, Lorissa Wilfong Holt's memoir of her two years in Hungary as a Peace Corps volunteer.

Please add $3 per book for postage and handling.
Idaho residents include 6% state sales tax in the amount of $0.90 per book.

Send check payable to:

Lorissa Holt
2186 Tanglewood Lane
Emmett ID 83617

Print Name_____

Address_____

City_____State____ Zip_____

I Remember . . . $15.00 x _____# books =_____

A Gift of Life $15.00 x _____# books =_____

Postage and Handling $3 x _____ # books = _____

Idaho Sales Tax $ 0.90 x _____ # books = _____

Enclosed is my check/money order for the total amount of

$_____

To order by phone or for bulk discount prices, please call:
(208) 365-6361 or email bwholt@clearwire.net

Please photocopy this page if additional forms are needed.